<u>*Edited Book*</u>

SCIENTIFIC ADVANCEMENTS IN CURRENT AGRICULTURAL RESEARCH

Editors

Dr. P. Sivasakthivelan
Department of Agricultural Microbiology, Faculty of Agriculture, Annamalai University, Annamalai Nagar, Tamil Nadu, India.

Dr. T. Uma Maheswari
Department of Horticulture, Faculty of Agriculture, Annamalai University, Annamalai Nagar, Tamil Nadu, India.

Dr. P. Saranraj
Department of Microbiology, Sacred Heart College (Autonomous), Tirupattur, Tamil Nadu, India.

Published by

JPS Scientific Publications
India

Published by

JPS Scientific Publications, Tamil Nadu, India.
E.mail: jpsscientificpublications@gmail.com
Website: www.jpsscientificpublications.com

Published in India.

International Standard Book Number (ISBN): 978-81-947154-7-4

JPS Scientific Publications also publishes its books in a variety of Electronic formats. Some content that appears in print may not be available in Electronic formats. For more information visit our publication website www.jpsscientificpublications.com

SAR is a distinct signal transduction pathway that plays an important role in the ability of plants to defend themselves against pathogens. SAR requires the signal molecule salicylic acid and is associated with accumulation of pathogenesis related proteins, which are thought to contribute to resistance. (Schuhegger *et al.* 2006). Example: *Streptomyces bikiniensis* HD-087 were able to induce systemic resistance in cucumber against *Fusarium wilt*, caused by *Fusarium oxysporum* f. sp. *cucumerinum.*

e) Hyperparasitism

Parasitism is the direct competitive interaction between two organisms in which one organism is gaining nutrients from the other. If the host is also a parasite, e.g., a plant pathogen, the interaction is defined as hyperparasitism. This kind of interaction is often observed between fungi. Several fungi and bacteria exhibit hyperparasitism on several other pathogenic fungi, in which they feed on the pathogenic microbes. A *S. griseus* strain has been reported to parasitize *Colletotrichum lindemuthianum* (common bean) and showed growth on its hyphae surface. The strain also showed internal parasitism of host hyphae, which resulted in the formation of several blebs. Cell walls of the parasitized *C. lindemuthianum* hyphae degenerated having a sponge-like texture and holes.

d) Siderophore production

Iron is a vital nutrient for almost all forms of life including plants and soil microorganisms. In the aerobic environment, iron occurs principally as Fe^{3+} in insoluble hydroxides and oxyhydraoxides form, thus making it generally inaccessible to both plants and microorganisms. Siderophores are low molecular weight high affinity iron chelators produced by many microorganisms, including actinomycetes, to scavenge ferric iron forming ferric- siderophore complexes which are shuttled back into the cells via active transport mechanisms. Streptomyces species are known to produce hydroxamate-type siderophores, which inhibit the growth of phytopathogens by limiting iron in rhizosphere soil. Siderophore compounds are potential plant growth promoters and disease suppressers. Jog *et al.* (2012) suggested that strains *Streptomyces rochei*, *Streptomyces carpinensis* and *Streptomyces thermolilacinus* have the ability to produce siderophores on CAS agar medium.

e) Hydrogen cyanide production

Hydrogen cyanide production plays a precious role in disease suppression and induces plant growth promotion directly or synergistically. It has been identified that certain endophytic *Streptomyces* species have been known to produce HCN, a

volatile antifungal compound, which contributes to the suppression of *Fusarium* disease and promotes plant growth. (Aydi-Benabdallah *et al.*, 2016).

f) Biocontrol agent

Actinobacteria exhibit several mechanisms of pathogen suppression and plant growth promotion. In order to utilize these activities of actinobacteria in sustainable agriculture for crop protection and production, formulation of the actinobacteria is necessary. Formulation is the process of mixing microbes or microbial products such as antibiotic secondary metabolites and cell wall-degrading enzymes with inert materials amended with nutritional supplements (in case of live microbes) to enhance their activity and viability during storage and field application. Several researchers attributed the inconsistency and failure of biocontrol agents under field conditions to the lack of proper formulation of the biocontrol agents (Macagnan *et al.* 2006). The type of formulation depends on the nature of the biocontrol agent (either live microbe or microbial products), site of application (soil, seed treatment, or foliar application), stability, and delivery at the site of action and the target pathogen (Sabaratnam and Traquair 2002). Traditionally, biocontrol formulations were prepared as liquids or powders (Schisler *et al.* 2004). Dry formulations (granules or powders) are generally preferred because of extended shelf life, easy transportation and storage, which can be suspended in liquid (oil, water, or oil in water emulsion) at the time of application (Sabaratnam and Traquair 2002).

Several commercial products derived from actinobacteria are available for use in crop protection and growth promotion

Application	Product Name	Active Ingredient	Control	Target pest
Fungicide	Actinovate® *AG*	*S.lydicus* WYEC108	Tree fruits, berries, and melons, vegetables including leafy vegetables, root crops, cole crops, peppers, and tomatoes.	Root decay fungi such as Fusarium, Rhizoctonia, Pythium, Phytophthora and powdery mildew and other fungal pathogens
	Actinovate® *SP*	*S.lydicus* WYEC108		
	Micro 108 ® soluble	*S.lydicus* WYEC108		
	Action Iron ®	*S.lydicus* WYEC108		
	Mycostop ®	*S. griseoviridis* strain K61		
Insecticide	Proclaim, Volex (Emamectin benzoate). Abba, Agri-mek, Termictine5% (Abamectin)	*Streptomyces avermitilis*	Brinjal, tomato, cauliflower and root crops	Lepidopteran larvae like helicoverpa, Dimond back moth, termite control and thrips etc.
	Milbeknock (Milbemectin)	*Streptomyces hygroscopicus*		

	Traer®, laser®, Conserve®, Entrust®, Spintor® (Spinosad)	*Saccharopolyspora spinosa*		
Bactericide	Agrimycin	*Streptomyces griseus*	Tomato, pepper, French bean, potato, beans and crucifers etc.	To control bacterial leaf spot, Hollow blight, bacterial rots of tubers and as a seed disinfectant in bacterial pathogens of beans.
	Phytomycin			
	Ortho-streptomycin			

g) Abiotic Stress Management

Biotic and abiotic stresses often limit plant productivity. These stresses induce the production of ethylene in plants, which negatively modulate plant growth. PGPR are renowned for their growth-enhancing effects on several plants by various mechanisms. One such mechanism is the production of an enzyme called 1-aminocyclopropane-1-carboxylate (ACC) deaminase that converts ACC, the precursor of ethylene in plants, into ammonia and α- ketobutyrate, thereby lowering stress-ethylene level and enhance plant growth. Many researchers have found that isolates *Streptomyces niveus, Streptomyces rochei, Streptomyces pada, Streptomyces coelicolor, Streptomyces olivaceus*, and *Streptomyces geysiriensis* may play a vital role in alleviating salinity and drought stress in various crops by changing the plants' physiological properties.

Actinomycetes mediated Abiotic Stress Management in Vegetables

Actinomycetes	Crops	Stress	Observed Effects	References
Streptomyces sp. PGPA39	Tomato	Salinity	Increase in plant biomass and chlorophyll content & a reduction in leaf proline content	Palaniyandi *et al.* (2014)
Citrococcus zhacaiensis B-4	Onion	Drought	Improved germination and seedling vigor	Selvakumar *et al.* (2015)

8. Conclusion

Actinomycetes have a great potential to be utilized in the bioinoculant industry apart from its use in pharmaceuticals. It can enhance the plant growth by producing growth regulators and other compounds and it is s well known for the production of antibiotics which add to its quality as biocontrol agent. Other features like production of cell wall degrading enzymes and induced systemic resistance can

also be useful in targeting new plant pathogens and will add to the campaign of green and sustainable agriculture.

9. References

1) Aydi-Benabdallah, R., Jabnoun-Khireddine, H., Nefzi, A., Mokni-Tlili, S., Daami-Remadi, M., 2016. Endophytic bacteria from *Datura metel* for plant growth promotion and bioprotection against *Fusarium* wilt in tomato. Biocontrol Sci. Technol. 26, 1139–1165.

2) Dakora FD, Phillips DA (2002) Root exudates as mediators of mineral acquisition in low-nutrient environments. Plant Soil 245:35–47.

3) El-Tarabily, K.A., Nassar, A.H., Hardy, G.E.S.J., Sivasithamparam, K., 2009. Plant growth promotion and biological control of Pythium aphanidermatum, a pathogen of cucumber, by endophytic actinomycetes. J. Appl. Microbiol. 106, 13–26.

4) Etebarian H R.2006.Evaluation of *Streptomyces* strains for biological control of charcoal stem rot of melon caused by *Macrophomina phaseolina*. Plant Pathology J.5(1): 83-87.

5) Gadelhak G., A Khaled, Y El-Tarabily and K Fatma. 2005. Insect control using chitinolytic soil actinomycetes as bio-control agents. Internl. J. Agri. And Biology. 7(4): 85.

6) Goodfellow, M. and Williams, ST. (1983). Ecology of actinomycetes. *Ann. Rev.*

7) Goudjal Y, Zamoum M, Meklat A, Sabaou N, Mathieu F, Zitouni A (2015) Plant growth-promoting potential of endosymbiotic actinobacteria isolated from sand truffles (Terfezia leonis Tul.) of the Algerian Sahara. Ann Microbiol. doi:10.1007/s13213-015-1085-2.

8) Hemant J. Patil, Alok K. Srivastava, Dhananjaya P. Singh, Bhushan L. Chaudhari, Dilip K. Arora.2011. Actinomycetes mediated biochemical responses in tomato (*Solanum lycopersicum*) enhances bioprotection against *Rhizoctonia solani*. Crop Protection 30: 1269 - 1273.

9) Jog, R., Nareshkumar, G., Rajkumar, S., 2012. Plant growth promoting potential and soil enzyme production of the most abundant *Streptomyces* spp. from wheat rhizosphere. J. Appl. Microbiol. 113, 1154–1164.

10) Khucharoenphaisan K, K. Rodbangpong, P. Saengpaen and K. Sinma.2016. Exploration on Soil Actinomycetes Against *Phytophthora* sp. Causing Root Rot of Cassava and Plant Growth Promoting Activities. J. Plant Sci., 11:38-44.

11) Lin L, Xu X (2013) Indole-3-acetic acid production by endophytic *Streptomyces* sp. En-1 isolated from medicinal plants. Curr Microbiol 67:209–217

12) Lin YB, Wang XY, Li HF, Wang NN, Wang HX, Tang M, Wei GH (2011) *Streptomyces zinciresistens* sp. nov., a zinc-resistant actinomycete isolated from soil from a copper and zinc mine. Int J Syst Evol Microbiol 61:616–620.

13) Merzaeva OV, Shirokikh IG (2010) The production of auxins by the endophytic bacteria of winter rye. Appl Biochem Microbiol 46: 44 - 50.

14) Mohandas S, Poovarasan S, Panneerselvam P, Saritha B, Upreti KK, Kamal R, Sita T (2013) Guava (*Psidium guajava* L.) rhizosphere *Glomus mosseae* spores harbour actinomycetes with growth-promoting and antifungal attributes. Sci Hortic. 150: 371 – 376.

15) Naglaa Hassan, Satoko Nakasuji, Mohsen Mohamed Elsharkawy, Hushna Ara Naznin, Masaharu Kubota, Hammad Ketta, and Masafumi Shimizu1. 2017. Biocontrol Potential of an Endophytic *Streptomyces* sp. Strain MBCN152-1 against *Alternaria brassicicola* on Cabbage Plug Seedlings. Microbes Environ. 32(2): 133 - 141.

16) Pal KK, Gardener BM. (2006). Biological control of plant pathogens. Plant Health Instructor. doi:10.1094/PHI-A-2006-1117-02

17) Palaniyandi, S.A., Damodharan, K., Yang, S.H., Suh, J.W. (2014). *Streptomyces* sp. strain PGPA39 alleviates salt stress and promotes growth of 'Micro Tom' tomato plants. J. Appl. Microbiol. 117: 766–773.

18) Rajeswari, M and Ramakrishnan, S. (2015). Influence of *Streptomyces fradiae* against Root knot nematode *Meloidogyne incognita* in Tomato. Research Journal of Agriculture and Forestry Sciences, 3(1): 6 - 11.

19) Sabaratnam, S and Traquair, J. A. (2002). Formulation of a *Streptomyces* biocontrol agent for the suppression of *Rhizoctonia* damping-off in tomato transplants. Biol. Control, 23: 245 - 253.

20) Sahu, M. K., K. Sivakumar, T. Thangaradjou and L. Kannan. (2007). Phosphate solubilising actinomycetes in the estuarine environment: An inventory. J. Environ. Biology, 28(4): 798.

21) Sarwar, A., Latif, Z., Zhang, S., Zhu, J., Zechel, D. L and Bechthold, A. (2018) Biological control of Potato Common Scab with rare Isatropolone C compound produced by Plant Growth Promoting *Streptomyces* A1RT. Front. Microbiol. 9: 1126.

22) Scherlach, K and Hertweck, C. (2009) Triggering cryptic natural product biosynthesis in microorganisms. Org. Biomol. Chem. 7(9): 1753 – 1760.

23) Schisler, D. A., Slininger, P. J., Behle, R. W and Jackson, M. A. (2004). Formulation of *Bacillus* spp. for biological control of plant diseases. Phytopathology, 94: 1267 – 1271.

24) Schuhegger R, Ihring A, Gantner S, Bahnweg G, Knappe C, Vogg G, Hutzler P, Schmid M, Breusegem FV, Eberl L, Hartmann A and Langebartels C. (2006). Induction of systemic resistance in tomato by N-acyl-L-homoserine lactone-producing rhizosphere bacteria. Plant Cell Environ., 29: 909 – 918.

25) Selvakumar G, Bhatt RM, Upreti KK, Bindu GH, Shweta K (2015). *Citricoccus zhacaiensis* B-4 (MTCC 12119) a novel osmotolerant plant growth promoting *Actinobacterium* enhances onion (*Allium cepa* L.) seed germination under osmotic stress condition. World J Microbiol Biotechnol., 31: 833 – 839.

26) Solans, M., Vobis, G., Cassan, F., Luna, V., Wall, L.G. (2011). Production of phytohormones by root-associated saprophytic actinomycetes isolated from the actinorhizal plant *Ochetophila trinervis*. World J. Microbiol. Biotechnol., 27: 2195 – 2202.

27) Sreevidya, M., Gopalakrishnan, S., Kudapa, H and Varshney, R. K. (2016). Exploring PGP actinomycetes from vermicompost and rhizosphere soil for yield enhancement in chickpea. Braz. J. Microbiol., 47: 85 – 95.

28) Valdés M, Pérez NO, Estrada-de Los Santos P, Caballero-Mellado J, Peña-Cabriales JJ, Normand P and Hirsch AM. (2005). Non-*Frankia* actinomycetes isolated from surface-sterilized roots of *Casuarina equisetifolia* fix nitrogen. Appl. Environ. Microbiol., 71: 460 – 466.

29) Yacine Goudjal, Miyada Zamoum, Nasserdine Sabaou, Florence Mathieu and Abdelghani Zitouni. (2016). Potential of endophytic *Streptomyces* spp. for biocontrol of *Fusarium* root rot disease and growth promotion of tomato seedlings. Biocontrol Science and Technology, 26(12): 1691 - 1705.

30) Yamaura M, Uchiumi T, Higashi S, Abe M and Kucho K. (2010). Identification of *Frankia* genes induced under nitrogen-fixing conditions by suppression subtractive hybridization. Appl. Environ. Microbiol., 76: 1692 - 1694.

Scientific Advancements in Current Agricultural Research
ISBN: 978-81-947154-7-4
First Edition; 2020
Chapter – 2, Page: 16 - 26

2

BIOSTIMULANTS – A BOON TO VEGETABLE CULTIVATION

P. Madhanakumari and V. M. Priyadarshini

Department of Horticulture, Faculty of Agriculture, Annamalai University, Annamalai Nagar, Tamilnadu, India.

Abstract

In the last thirty years, numerous scientific revolutions have been planned to improve the ecological balance of agricultural production methods, *via* a considerable decrease of inorganic compounds like pesticides, synthetic plant growth hormones and fertilizers. A favourable and environment sustainable modernization should be the practice of normal Plant Biostimulants (PBs) which augment flowering, plant evolution, fruit formation, crop output and efficient nutrient mobilization, and ability to endure a varied array of abiotic stressors. The research interest on plant biostimulants in vegetable production is gradually increasing and several reports highlight the beneficial effects that such products may have not only on crop performance but also on the quality of the final product. Moreover, numerous products with biostimulatory activity are being developed which need further evaluation under variable growing conditions and different crops. This review provides an overview of the main findings of the study, while discussing the practical applications that biostimulants may have in the production of vegetable crops, aiming to increase the yield and the quality of the final produce and improve crop tolerance to abiotic stressors.

Keywords: Biostimulants, Mechanisms, Growth, Yield, Quality and NUE

1. Introduction

Modern agriculture needs to review and broaden its practices and business models, by integrating opportunities coming from different adjacent sectors and value chains, including the biobased industry, in a fully circular economy strategy (Colla and Rouphael, 2015). Biobased products such as biostimulants represent a sustainable, efficient technology or complement to their synthetic counterparts (i.e., agrochemicals) to improve nutrient use efficiency and secure yield stability of agricultural and horticulture crops under optimal and sub-optimal conditions (Fiorentino *et al.*, 2018). Biostimulants are excerpts acquired from organic raw ingredients having bioactive composites. Plant biostimulant is well-defined as components, with the exception of nutrients and pesticides, which, when subjected to plants, seeds or growing substrates in precise formulations have the ability to modify the physiological actions of plants in such way that caters prospective edge to growth, development and stress response (Du Jardin, 2012). Many diverse natural substances and chemical derivatives of natural or synthetic compounds as well as beneficial microorganisms are catalogued as plant biostimulants including: (i) humic substances; (ii) vegetal or animal-based protein hydrolysates; (iii) macro- and micro-algal extracts; (iv) silicon; (v) arbuscular mycorrhizal fungi (AMF); and (vi) plant growth promoting rhizobacteria (PGPR) belonging to the genus *Azotobacter, Azospirillum* and *Rizhobium* spp. (Battacharya *et al.*, 2015; Canellas *et al.*, 2015; Ruzzi *et al.*, 2015; Colla *et al.*, 2017; Chiaiese *et al.*, 2018). The application of plant biostimulants is an innovative environmental friendly approach towards sustainable crop production which faces several limitations such as water scarcity, depletion of natural resources, environmental stressors and climate change (Rouphael *et al.*, 2018). The use of biostimulants is indicated in high added value crops such as vegetable crops and intensified cropping systems due to the high cost for most of the commercially available products (Szparaga *et al.*, 2019). The present review paper compiles many aspects that are helpful to the scientific community, extension specialists, and commercial enterprises to better elucidate the causal/functional mechanism of microbial and non-microbial biostimulants.

2. Types of Biostimulants

Humic acids and Fulvic acids

Humic substances (HS) are the innate components of the soil organic matter which is not only the consequent of the degradation of plant, animal and residue of microorganism, but the metabolic products of soil microorganisms utilizing such degraded components. In fact, they are the ultimate yield of microbial breakdowns and chemical deterioration of dead flora and fauna in soils (Asli and Peter, 2010).

Humic substances have been acknowledged as indispensable contributors to soil fertility, acting on physical, physico-chemical, chemical and biological properties of the soil. In plants they play a major role in regulating accessibility of nutrients, diffusion of oxygen and carbon between the troposphere and the soil and lethal chemicals alteration and transport (Pilon-Smiths *et al.*, 2009). Fulvic acid can be observed as organic portion of soil, which can dissolve in alkaline as well as in acidic medium (Schiavon *et al.*, 2010). Fulvic acid has higher total acidity, higher carboxyl groups and more adsorption and cation exchange capacities as compared to humic acid (Bocanegra *et al.*, 2006).

Protein hydrolysates and other Nitrogen containing compounds

Amino-acids and peptides mixtures are procured by the chemical and enzymatic protein degradation of by-products from agro-based industries, from both plant sources (crop residues) as well as animal wastes (e.g. collagen, epithelial tissues) (Calvo *et al.*, 2014; Halpern *et al.*, 2015). It has direct impacts on plants comprise nodulation of N uptake and acclimatization, by the regulating of enzymes implicated in N metabolism and structural genes, and by stimulating the signalling pathway of N acquirement in roots. They regulate the TCA cycle enzymes, effects C and N metabolisms. Complex protein and tissue hydrolysates are influenced by the hormonal activities (Colla *et al.*, 2014).

Seaweed extracts and Botanicals

Seaweeds or macroalgae are aquatic plants belonging to the plant kingdom Thallophyta. These organisms are often considered as an under-utilized bio-resource, while many species have been utilized as food, industrial gums, and in therapeutic and botanical applications for centuries (Eef *et al.,* 2018). The polyanionic compounds helps in the fixation and exchange of cations, fixation of heavy metals and soil remediation. In plants, they act as fertilisers, beside their other roles on the effects on seed germination, plant establishment, growth and development which is related with hormonal effects, which is regarded as main reasons of biostimulation activity on crop plants (Pamela *et al.*, 2014).

Chitosan and other Biopolymers

Chitosan, a deacetylated product of the biopolymer chitin, synthesized through both naturally and artificially. Different and controlled sizes of poly and oligomers are being utilized in various foods, cosmetic, medical and agricultural sectors. The physiological response of chitosan oligomers in crops are not only the consequent of the abilities of this polycationic substance to associate with a broad categories of cellular components such as DNA, plasma membrane and cell wall

constituents, but owing to associate with a unique receptors related to activation of gene involve defence mechanism, a way similar to plant defence elicitors (El Hadrami *et al.*, 2010; Hadwiger *et al.*, 2013; Katiyar *et al.*, 2015).

Panchagavya

Sivakumar *et al.* (2014) stated that Panchagavya provides macronutrients, essential micronutrients, many vitamins, required amino acids, growth-promoting substances and beneficial microorganisms which improves plant growth. Suchitra Rakesh *et al.* (2017) revealed that Panchagavya contains *Azotobacter*, *Azospirillum* and Phosphobacteria. Panchagavya contains microorganisms in addition to nutrients that help in improving plant growth, metabolic activities, and resistance to pests and diseases. A wonder medicine named Panchagavya (a combination of cow urine, milk, dung, ghee, and curd) was offered by Maharishi Dhanvantari to mankind. It helps to enhance the biological efficiency of crop plants and enhances the quality of fruits and vegetables (Naresh *et al.*, 2018).

3. Applications of Biostimulants

Implications on growth and yield characters of plants

The enhancement of plant development process along with crop yield as a result of application of PBs has been generally correlated to the activity of signalling biologically active elements in the primary and secondary metabolisms (Calvo *et al.*, 2014). Vasantharaja *et al.* (2019) observed that 3 % foliar spray of brown seaweed (*Sargassum swartzii*) was found to significantly improve the growth characters like shoot length, number of leaves in cowpea (*Vigna unguiculata* L.). The root growth stimulatory effect was more when seaweed extract was applied at the early stages of growth, where the response was similar to that of auxin, an important root growth-promoting hormone. Seaweed extract contains plant hormones such as auxins, cytokinin, abscisic acid and amino acids which are required for the physical and physiological development of plants. Kumar *et al.* (2019) on cluster bean (*Cyamopsistetra gonoloba* L.) revealed that organic manures increased the plant height, number of leaves, number of pods plant[-1] and yield in plants when treated with 25 t of farm yard manure + 3 % Panchagavya which was equally effective as that of RDF + TNAU pulse powder. Panchagavya provides macronutrients, essential micronutrients, many vitamins, required amino acids, growth-promoting substances and beneficial microorganisms which improves plant growth (Sivakumar *et al.,* 2014). Khan *et al.* (2018) reported that various combinations of chitosan and humic acid significantly improved the plant growth and yield parameters in Pea Cv. Meteor. The results indicated that 80 mg L[-1] of chitosan and 2 g L[-1] of humic acid gave the best results in enhancing different growth and yield attributes like the

Chapter - 2

number of pods and pod length. They also contributed to stress tolerance. Chitin and chitosan; evidently used as unique receptors and signalling pathways. They are the major players in responding to stress stimulus as well as in the developmental regulations, amongst the cellular consequences of the attaching of chitosan to approximately definite cell receptors, hydrogen peroxide aggregation and Ca^{2+} efflux into the cell were shown, seems to cause an enormous functional change.

Implications of Biostimulants for enhancing quality of produce

The microbial and non-microbial plant Biostimulants application have the capacity to alter plant's metabolism both primary and secondary (Colla *et al.*, 2015) which results in the synthesis as well as build-up of antioxidant compounds (i.e., secondary metabolites) which are vital for human nutrition. This treatment also cause a considerable boost in tomato fruit quality such as antioxidant capacity, total soluble sugars, carotenoids (lycopene, lutein, and β-carotene), total polyphenols and flavonoids contents along with mineral composition (P, K, Ca, Mg, Fe, Mn, and Zn).Concerning the implications of microbial plant biostimulants on improving produce quality, (Chandrasekaran *et al.*, 2019) reported that the inoculation of PGPR strain, Bacillus subtilis CBR05 induced a significant increase in tomato quality in terms of carotenoids profile (β-carotene and lycopene). El-Tanahy *et al.* (2012) found that chitosan at 5 % along with inorganic fertilizer had the best effect on seeds quality (total protein, total carbohydrates N, P and K) in vegetable cowpea. Application of Panchagavya in brinjal has found to have a positive impact on the total phenolic content (Suchitra Rakesh *et al.*, 2017). Furthermore, Haplern *et al.* (2015) conducted an experiment on two *Brassica* species: *Brassica campestris* and *Brassica juncea* and studied the effect of PAR (photosynthetically active radiation) (low or high), phosphate (low or high), and phosphite (low, optimal or high), and their interlinkage on the content of glucosinolates, flavonoids, and nitrate. They highlighted that the addition of phosphite in the nutrient medium may cause an enhancement in phosphate deficiency; thus it stimulates the biosynthesis as well as aggregation of several target flavonoids and glucosinolates as a probable defence system to cope with nutrient stress.

Impacts of Biostimulants on physical characteristics

Biostimulants also have an influence on the mechanical properties i.e., the firmness of vegetables, colour etc. Depending on the type, biostimulants may cause the stiffening of cell walls, thereby reducing their extensibility (Tarantino *et al.*, 2018). Biostimulants that increase the flexibility of cell walls at the same time extend the shelf-life of fruits and vegetables for consumption and facilitate their storage. Biostimulants based on carboxylic, humic, and fulvic acids and also the biopolymers

of polysaccharides increased the mechanical strength (Tarantino *et al.*, 2018). An important visual feature that proves the quality of the fruit is colour. The colour of the fruit is substantially influenced by the anthocyanin content. Weber *et al.* 2018examined the content of anthocyanins in strawberries treated with *Ascophyllum nodosum* extract with silicon. Vegetables treated with a biostimulator were characterized by a higher content of anthocyanins in the initial fruiting period, therefore, they were red than the control fruits. Seaweed extract increased the relative water content of the leaves from 76 % to 82 %. The surface area of the leaf was also increased by 16 % (foliar spray), 21 % (biostimulant in the irrigation system), and 38 % (biostimulant in the irrigation system and in a spray). Increasing the area and turgor of the leaf led to an increase in the intensity of photosynthesis and improved the conditions for growing spinach under stress conditions (Xu *et al.*, 2015).

Impacts on abiotic stress tolerance

Abiotic stresses, in particular drought, salinity, heat stress, hypoxia and nutrient deficiency, are responsible for 60 – 70 % of yield gap, dictated by global climate changes (Rouphael *et al.*, 2018). In their review paper, Bulgari and co-workers summarized the biostimulants literature (humic substances, seaweed extracts, protein hydrolysates, amino acids and beneficial microorganisms) regarding their use on vegetables, focusing on their application and mode of actions to counteract the most common abiotic stresses: cold/chilling stress, heat, salinity, drought stress and nutrient deficiency. In addition to the categorized plant biostimulants. Arnao *et al.* (2019) proposed the dual use of melatonin (N-acetyl-5-methoxytryptamine) as plant protector and biostimulant. In their review paper, they discussed the different legal aspects to categorize this natural substance as potential biostimulant at the European level. They summarized the studies of different responses of melatonin in different plant species and under diverse stress conditions by reporting the observed effects/mechanisms. The application of four commercial biostimulants containing protein hydrolysates, humic acid and especially brown seaweed extracts (*A. nodosum*) were found to mitigate the negative effects of water stress (70 % or 50 % of the container substrate capacity) on potted mint by increasing the antioxidant activity of key enzymes such as catalase and superoxide dismutase and by reducing the H_2O_2 accumulation in leaf tissue (Elansary *et al.*, 2019). The positive consequences of biostimulants may be correlated to various physio-chemical processes such as (i) reduced membrane lipid peroxidation, (ii) enhanced chlorophyll content, (iii) better antioxidant activities and (iv) an improved afflux and compartmenlizing the intracellular ions.

Non-microbial and microbial plant biostimulants may positively influence nutrient use efficiency (NUE), in particular nitrogen (N) by enhancing root system architecture and soil exploration as well as increasing macro- and micronutrient solubilization that can result in an increase in NUE (De Pascale *et al.*, 2018; Carillo *et al.*, 2019). Di Mola *et al.* (2019) demonstrated that foliar application of protein hydrolysates and sea weed extract based biostimulants is considered as a sustainable approach to increase baby lettuce productivity and NUE in greenhouse. Interestingly, the foliar application of vegetal-based biostimulants incurred a significant increase in N uptake and N use efficiencies in leafy vegetables (19 % and 18 %, respectively, for baby spinach and 50 % and 73 %, respectively, for lamb's lettuce).The improved agronomic feedbacks of H applied tomato were related to the improvements of root architecture that resulted in better N uptake and translocation. Furthermore, in suboptimal N level, PH treatment enhanced the expression of genes encoding for amino acid transporter and ferredoxin-glutamate synthases and glutamine synthetase in roots, which are reported to be necessary in N metabolism (Savvas *et al.*, 2015). Rouphael and co-workers concluded that, based on the improved fresh yield and NUE in greenhouse lettuce plants, treatment with plant biostimulants improved not only the chlorophyll synthesis and mineral status but also the synthesis and accumulation of antioxidant metabolites that were responsible for reactivating the photosynthetic activity and consequently the agronomic performance.

4. Conclusion – The future of Biostimulant Science

The use of biostimulants on a commercial scale would limit the amount of mineral fertilizers introduced into the environment, thus reducing the pollution of soils, water, and air. This is especially important in the case of global warming. Numerous experiments have suggested that linking numerous biostimulants could offer steady effects as compared with their individual treatment. As biostimulating effects are distinctly species-specific and product-specific and our knowledge of one biostimulant or about single plant species can't be sprightly transfered to another biostimulant or another plant species. In order to expand both basic and applied science regarding the efficacy of biostimulants for a particular plant species, it is necessary to perform a broad spectrum research on this species, with a variety of products, treatments, growth stages, etc. PBs such as natural substances and microbial inoculants. Although plant biostimulants appear to be a novel and potential category of agricultural inputs complementing synthetic fertilizers, there is an urgent need among the research community and fertilizer industries to elucidate the molecular and physiological mechanisms which will definitely facilitate the

diffusion of these bio-products in the agricultural sector. Finally, Giovannini *et al.* (2020) suggested that, in the near future, transcriptomics research should be adopted as an integrated tool to identify the best synergistic combinations of AMF and associated bacterial communities able to enhance resources use efficiency, plant resilience and boosting nutraceutical compounds in plant species.

5. References

1) Arnao, M.B and J. Hernández-Ruiz. 2019. Melatonin as a Chemical Substance or as Phytomelatonin Rich-Extracts for Use as Plant Protector and/or Biostimulant in Accordance with EC Legislation. Agronomy.9: 570.

2) Asli, S., and M. Neumann Peter. 2010. Rhizosphere humic acid interacts with root cell walls to reduce hydraulic conductivity and plant development. Plant Soil. 336:313– 322.

3) Battacharyya, D., M. Z. Babgohari, P. Rathor and B. Prithiviraj. 2015. Seaweed extracts as biostimulants in horticulture. Sci. Hortic. 196: 39–48.

4) Bocanegra, A., J. Benedi and F. Sanchez-Muniz. 2006. Differential effects of konbu and nori seaweed dietary supplementation on liver glutathione status in normo- and hypercholesterolaemic growing rats. Bri. J.Nutr. 95:696–702.

5) Calvo, P., L. Nelson and J. W. Kloepper. 2014. Agricultural uses of plant biostimulants. Plant Soil. 383:3-41.

6) Canellas, L.P., F. L. Olivares, N. O. Aguiar, D. L. Jones, A. Nebbioso, P. Mazzei and A. Piccolo. 2015.Humic and fulvic acids as biostimulants in horticulture. Sci. Hortic. 196: 15–27.

7) Carillo, P., G. Colla, G. M. Fusco, E. Dell'Aversana, C. El-Nakhel, M. Giordano, A. Pannico, E. Cozzolino, M. Mori and H. Reynaud. 2019. Morphological and Physiological Responses Induced by Protein Hydrolysate-Based Biostimulant and Nitrogen Rates in Greenhouse Spinach. Agronomy. 9: 450.

8) Chandrasekaran, M., S. C. Chun, J. W. Oh, M. Paramasivan, R. K. Saini and J. J. Sahayarayan. 2019. *Bacillus subtilis* CBR05 for Tomato (*Solanum lycopersicum*) Fruits in South Korea as a Novel Plant Probiotic Bacterium (PPB): Implications from Total Phenolics, Flavonoids, and Carotenoids Content for Fruit Quality. Agronomy. 9: 838.

9) Chiaiese, P., G. Corrado, G. Colla, M. C.Kyriacou and Y. Rouphael. 2018. Renewable Sources of Plant Biostimulation: Microalgae as a Sustainable Means to Improve Crop Performance. Front. Plant Sci. 9: 9.

10) Colla, G., Y. Rouphael, R. Canaguier, E. Svecova and M. Cardarelli. 2014.Biostimulant action of a plant-derived protein hydrolysate produced through enzymatic hydrolysis. Front. Plant Sci.5:1–6.

11) Colla, G., L. Hoagland, M. Ruzzi, M. Cardarelli, P. Bonini, R. Canaguier and Y. Rouphael. 2017.Biostimulant Action of Protein Hydrolysates: Unraveling Their Effects on Plant Physiology and Microbiome. Front. Plant Sci. 8: 2202.

12) Colla, G., S. Nardi, M. Cardarelli, A. Ertani, L. Lucini, R. Canaguier and Y. Rouphael. 2015 Protein hydrolysates as biostimulants in horticulture. Sci. Hortic. 196: 28–38.

13) Colla, G. and Y. Rouphael. 2015.Biostimulants in horticulture. Sci. Hortic. 196: 1–2.

14) De Pascale, S., Y. Rouphael and G. Colla. 2018. Plant biostimulants: Innovative tool for enhancing plant nutrition in organic farming. Eur. J. Hortic. Sci. 82: 277–285.

15) Di Mola, I., E. Cozzolino, L. Ottaiano, M. Giordano, Y. Rouphael, G. Colla and M. Mori. 2019. Effect of Vegetal- and Seaweed Extract-Based Biostimulants on Agronomical and Leaf Quality Traits of Plastic Tunnel-Grown Baby Lettuce under Four Regimes of Nitrogen Fertilization. Agronomy. 9: 571.

16) Du Jardin, P. 2012. The science of plant biostimulants- A bibliographic analysis. Adhoc Study Report to the European Commission DGENTR.

17) Eef, B., D. Marlies, K. Van Swam, A. Veen and L. Burger. 2018. Identification of the seaweed biostimulant market (Phase1); The North Sea Farm Foundation: AD Den Haag, The Netherlands.

18) El Hadrami, A., L. R. Adam, I. El Hadrami and F. Daayf. 2010. Chitosan in plant protection. Mar Drugs. 8:968-987.

19) Elansary, H.O, E. A. Mahmoud, D. O. El-Ansary and M. Mattar. 2019. Effects of Water Stress and Modern Biostimulants on Growth and Quality Characteristics of Mint. Agronomy. 10: 6.

20) Fiorentino, N, V. Ventorino, S. L. Woo, O. Pepe, A. De Rosa, L. Gioia, I. Romano, N. Lombardi, M. Napolitano and G. Colla. 2018. Trichoderma-Based Biostimulants Modulate Rhizosphere Microbial Populations and Improve N Uptake Efficiency, Yield, and Nutritional Quality of Leafy Vegetables. Front. Plant Sci. 9: 9.

21) Giovannini, L., M. Palla, M. Agnolucci, L. Avio, C. Sbrana, A. Turrini and M. Giovannetti. 2020. Arbuscular Mycorrhizal Fungi and Associated Microbiota as Plant Biostimulants: Research Strategies for the Selection of the Best Performing Inocula. Agronomy. 10: 106.

22) Hadwiger, L. A. 2013. Multiple effects of chitosan on plant systems: Solid science or hype. Plant Sci.208:42-49.

23) Halpern, M., A. Bar-Tal, M. Ofek, D. Minz, T. Muller and U. Yermiyahu. 2015. The use of biostimulants for enhancing nutrient uptake. In: Sparks, D.L. (Ed.). Adv.Agron. 129:141–174.

24) Katiyar, D., A. Hemantaranjan and B. Singh. 2015. Chitosan as a promising natural compound to enhance potential physiological responses in plant: A review. Indian J. Plant Physiol.20:1-9.

25) Khan, R., N. Manzoor, A. Zia, I. Ahmad, A. Ullah, S. M. Shah, M. Naeem, S. Ali, I. H. Khan, D. Zia and S. Malik. 2018. Exogenous application of chitosan and humic acid effects on plant growth and yield of pea (*Pisumsativum*). Int. J. Biosci. 12(5): 43-50.

26) Kocira, S., A. Szparaga, M. Kubon, E. Czerwinska and T. Piskier. 2019. Morphological and Biochemical Responses of *Glycine max* (L.) Merr. to the Use of Seaweed Extract. Agronomy. 9: 93.

27) Kumar, A. T., E. Somasundaram and N. Thavaprakaash. 2019. Influence of organic manures on growth and yield of vegetable Cluster bean (*Cyamopsistetragonoloba* (L.) Taub.).J. Pharmacognosy and Phytochemistry. 8(3): 3331-3334.

28) Naresh, R. K., A. K. Shukla, M. Kumar, A. Kumar, R. K. Gupta and S. P. Vivek Singh. 2018. Cowpathy and Vedic Krishi to Empower Food and Nutritional Security and Improve Soil Health: A Review. J. Pharmacognosy and Phytochemistry. 7(1): 560-575.

29) Pamela, C., N. Louise and W. K. Joseph. 2014. Agricultural uses of plant biostimulants. Plant Soil.

30) Pilon-Smits, E. A. H., C. F. Quinn, W.Tapken, M. Malagoli and M. Schiavon. 2009. Physiological functions of beneficial elements. Curr. Opin. Plant Biol. 12:267-274.

31) Rouphael, Y. and G. Colla. 2018. Synergistic Biostimulatory Action: Designing the Next Generation of Plant Biostimulants for Sustainable Agriculture. Front. Plant Sci. 9: 9.

32) Ruzzi, M and R. Aroca. 2015. Plant growth-promoting rhizobacteria act as biostimulants in horticulture. Sci. Hortic. 196: 124–134.

33) Savvas, D and G. Ntatsi. 2015.Biostimulant activity of silicon in horticulture. Sci. Hortic. 2015, 196: 66–81.

34) Schiavon, M., D. Pizzeghello, A. Muscolo, S. Vaccaro, O. Francioso and S. Nardi. 2010. High molecular size humic substances enhance phenylpropanoidmetabolismin maize (*Zea mays* L.). J. Chem. Ecol.36:662–669.

35) Sivakumar, T. 2014. Review on Panchagavya. Int. J Adv. Res. Biol. Sci. 1:130-154.

36) Suchitra. R, S., B. Poonguzhali, S. Saranya, Suguna and K. Jothibasu. 2017. Effect of panchagavya on Growth and Yield of *Abelmoschusesculentus* cv. ArkaAnamika. Int. J Curr. Microbiol. App. Sci. 6(9): 3090-3097.

37) Tarantino, A., F. Lops, G. Disciglio and G. Lopriore. 2018. Effects of Plant Biostimulants on Fruit Set, Growth, Yield and Fruit Quality Attributes of 'Orange Rubis®' Apricot (*Prunusarmeniaca* L.) Cultivar in Two Consecutive Years. Sci. Hortic. 239: 26–34.

38) Vasantharaja, R., L. Stanley Abraham, D. Inbakandan, R. Thirugnanasambandam, T. Senthilvelan, S.K. Ayesha Jabeen and P. Prakash. 2019. Influence of seaweed extracts on growth, phytochemical contents and antioxidant capacity of cowpea (*Vignaunguiculata* L. Walp). Biocatal. Agric. Biotechnol. 17: 589-594

39) Weber, N., V. Schmitzer, J. Jakopic and F. Stampar. 2018. First Fruit in Season: Seaweed Extract and Silicon Advance Organic Strawberry (*Fragaria × Ananassa*Duch.) Fruit Formation and Yield. Sci. Hortic. 242: 103–109.

40) Xu, C. and D. I. Leskovar. 2015. Effects of *A. nodosum* Seaweed Extracts on Spinach Growth, Physiology and Nutrition Value under Drought Stress. Sci. Hortic. 183: 39–47.

41) El-Tanahy, A.M.M., A. R. Mahmoud, M. M. Abde-Mouty and A. H. Ali. 2012. Effect of Chitosan Doses and Nitrogen Sources on the Growth, Yield and Seed Quality of Cowpea. Aust. J. Basic Appl. Sci. 6(4): 115-121.

Scientific Advancements in Current Agricultural Research
ISBN: 978-81-947154-7-4
First Edition; 2020
Chapter – 3, Page: 27 - 38

3

ROLE OF BORON AND ZINC IN SOLANACEOUS VEGETABLES

S. Kamalakannan[1]*, S. Meena[1], S. Madhavan[1] and J. Nambi[2]

[1]Department of Horticulture, Faculty of Agriculture, Annamalai University, Annamalai Nagar, Tamil Nadu, India.
[2]Department of Agronomy, Faculty of Agriculture, Annamalai University, Annamalai Nagar, Tamil Nadu, India.

*Corresponding author: kamalhort@gmail.com

Abstract

Proper plant nutrition is essential for successful production of vegetable crops. Micronutrients are usually required in minute quantities, nevertheless, are vital to the growth of plants. Judicious use of micronutrients is essential for vegetable cultivation to get maximum yield of high-quality produce. Micronutrients like zinc and boron are essential for plant metabolism, nutrient regulation, chlorophyll synthesis, reproductive growth, flower retention, fruit and seed development. Boron is associated with the carbohydrate metabolism and reproductive phase of the plants along with photosynthesis or enzymatic activities.

Key words: Zinc, Boron, Tomato, Brinjal, Chilli and Potato.

1. Introduction

Micronutrients are needed in very little quantity but are very important for proper growth of plants (Mousavi, 2009). Like many other micronutrients zinc and boron are very important elements although required in very small quantity by plants for some specific and physiological functions performed by plants. Zinc is responsible for many enzymatic activities i.e., aldolase, peptidase, isomerase and

phosphohydrolase etc. (Rawat and Mathpal, 1984). Zinc and boron are responsible for enhancement of photosynthesis (Gupta, 1993). It is also responsible for the synthesis of tryptophan which is involved in the formation of Indole Acetic Acid (Marschner, 1995).

Zinc (Zn) is one of the eight essential micronutrients. It is needed by plants in small amounts, but yet crucial to plant development. In plants, it is a key constituent of many enzymes and proteins. It plays an important role in a wide range of processes, such as growth hormone production and internode elongation. Boron (B) is an essential and important micronutrient critical to the growth of all crops and it is required in small amounts. It plays a key role in a diverse range of plant functions including cell wall formation and stability, maintenance of structural and functional integrity of biological membranes, movement of sugar or energy into growing parts of plants, pollination and seed set. The various sources of zinc as stated by Ramrattan and Sharma (2005) is as follows

Name of the Compounds	Percentage of Zinc
Zinc sulphate heptahydrate ($ZnSo_4.7H_2O$)	21 %
Zinc sulphate monohydrate ($ZnSo_4.H_2O$)	33 %
Chelated zinc as Zn-EDTA	12 %
Zincated urea	2 %
Zincated phosphate	19.4 %
Zinc oxide	60 – 80 %
Zinc carbonate ($ZnCo_3$)	52 – 56 %
Zinc chloride ($ZnCl_2$)	48 – 50 %

2. Various forms of Zinc in soil

- *Mineral form*: Exist as zinc sulphides, zinc carbonates and zinc silicates.
- *Adsorbed form*: It is adsorbed on the surface of clays, oxide minerals, carbonates and organic matters.
- *Solution form*: In soil, solution of zinc exists as zinc ion and zinc hydroxide.

Organic complex form: Zinc forms stable complex with organic colloids. This form is readily available to plants.

3. Role of Zinc in Plant system

- *Low molecular weight complexes of zinc*: In plant leaves soluble zinc occurs mainly as anionic compound possibly associated with amino acid.
- *Carbohydrate metabolism*: During photosynthesis, zinc is a constituent of carbonic anhydrase enzyme, which have major role in carbon-di-oxide fixation.
- *Membrane integrity*: The role of zinc in maintaining the integrity of cellular membranes involving structural orientation of macromolecules and also maintenance of ion transport system.
- *Protein metabolism*: Zinc is necessary for the activity of RNA polymerase enzyme and it protects ribosomal RNA from attack by the enzyme ribonuclease.
- *Auxin metabolism*: Zinc is required for synthesis of auxin and synthesis of tryptophan which is precursor of auxin.

4. Importance of Zinc

Zinc is indispensable for normal growth and development of plants. It is effective for the synthesis of plant hormones like auxin and carbohydrate formation (Pankaj *et al.*, 2018). It plays a fundamental role in several critical functions in the cell such as protein metabolism, gene expression, structural and functional integrity of bio-membranes and photosynthetic metabolism (Sanju *et al.*, 2003). It is also a constituent of ribosomes and is essential for their structural integrity (Trivedi *et al.*, 2013). It promotes starch formation, seed maturation, production, enhances seed viability and seedling vigor. It is helpful in reproduction of certain plants and various enzymatic activities (Pandev *et al.*, 2016). Zinc nutrition in plants seems to play a major role in the resistance to salt in tomato. An adequate zinc (Zn) nutritional status improves salt stress tolerance, possibly, by affecting the structural integrity and controlling the permeability of root cell membranes and reduces excessive uptake of sodium by roots in saline conditions Haifa, (2018).

5. Importance of Boron

Boron plays an essential role in the growth and development of new cells in the meristemmatic region of plants. It is necessary for cell wall formation, development of fruit and seed. It helps in pollen formation, pollination and flowering of plants (Malek and Rahim, 2011). It also involves in metabolism and transport of carbohydrates, nucleic acid synthesis, root elongation, photosynthetic activities and water absorption in plant parts (Islam *et al.*, 2018). It increases the stability of plant

cells and involved in the reproductive phase of plants. Kaursidhu *et al.* (2019) reported the following sources of boron.

Name of the compounds	Percentage of Boron
Borax (Sodium tetraborate)	10.5 %
Boric acid	17.0 %
Disodium octaborate tetrahydrate	20 %

Guideline for critical, sufficient and toxic levels of plant nutrients

Element	Critical level	Sufficient level	Toxicity level
Zn (mg/kg)	15 - 20	20 - 250	>400
B (mg/kg)	<10.0	10 - 100	>100

6. Research findings on Solanaceous Vegetable Crops

a) Tomato

Zinc deficiency symptoms in Tomato

Tomato leaf shows an advanced case of interveinal necrosis. In the early stages of zinc deficiency the younger leaves become yellow and pitting develops in the interveinal upper surfaces of the mature leaves. As the deficiency progresses these symptoms develop into an intense interveinal necrosis but the main veins remain green, as in the symptoms of recovering iron deficiency.

Boron deficiency symptoms in Tomato

Boron deficiency symptoms generally appear in younger plants at the propagation stage slight interveinal chlorosis in older leaves followed by yellow to orange tinting in middle and older leaves. The leaves and stems are brittle and corky, split and swollen misshaped fruit.

A hydroponic study was conducted by Jeanine *et al.* (2003) at North Carolina state university, Raligh in tomato. Three treatments were used in this experiment viz., control, that is without using of boron, foliar applied boron at the rate of 1.87mg/lit of water and soil applied boron at the rate of 4 kg/ha. They observed that the highest crack point (55.4 N), concentric crack (0.79 Mg ha), radial crack (0.26) was recorded with soil applied boron at the rate of 4 kg/ha. Foliar and soil applied boron increased the fruit crack point compared to untreated plants and plants treated with foliar applied boron had less fruit with concentric and radial cracks than the control and soil applied with boron, these results suggested that boron may be important in reducing the incidence of fruit cracking.

Chapter - 3

A study undertaken by Davies *et al.*, (2003) on tomato showed that soil application of boron at the rate of 2 kg/ha was increasing the shelf life when compared to foliar application at the rate of 1.8 mg/lit of boron. On the other hand, without using of any boron that is control the defective fruit is maximum.

Gurumani *et al.*, (2012) conducted an experiment on the soil application of zinc and the results indicated that the zinc application significantly increased the leaf chlorophyll, sugar and protein concentrations over control except 5 mg of zinc/kg. The highest chlorophyll contents were achieved with 15 mg of zinc/kg followed by 10 and 5 mg of zinc/kg. Naz et al., (2012) reported that the maximum fruit set percentage (55.83) was obtained with 2.0 kg B ha. While minimum fruit set percentage (39.77) was recorded with control treatments.

In an experiment on tomato fruit set percentage of rio grand and rio figure cultivars, Mohip *et al.*, (2012) found significant effect on the fruit set percentage of tomato. However, 2kg of boron/ha resulted in maximum fruit set percentage in rio grand cultivar while lowest fruit set percentage was found with rio figure cultivar. So, the result clearly indicated that boron plays a vital role in fruit set percentage of tomato plants.

Meena *et al.* (2015) conducted an experiment on the improvement of growth, yield and quality of Tomato (*Solanum lycopersicum* L.) cv. Azard T-6 with foliar application of zinc and boron and suggested that the plant height was significantly increased with the application of boron 100 ppm and recorded maximum height 41.05 cm and 61.23 cm at 60 DAT and 90 DAT.

Ali *et al.* (2015) conducted a study on the effect of foliar application of zinc and boron on flower and fruit characters of BARI hybrid tomato 4x. The results revealed that the early flowering (49.3 days), maximum number of fruits per cluster (1.8) and number of fruits per plant (33.6), maximum fruit length (5.3 cm), fruit diameter (5.1 cm) were found in the treatment which received 12.5 ppm (Zinc sulphate) + 12.5 ppm (Boric acid) while control showed late flowering (55.5 days), minimum number of fruits per cluster and number of fruits per plant (1.6 and 29.4) respectively, and minimum fruit length and fruit diameter (3.7 cm and 3.6 cm respectively).

An investigation was carried out by Haleema *et al.* (2018) on tomato with different concentrations of boron and zinc at the rate of 0, 0.25, and 0.5 %, and were applied as foliar spray at 3 times. The first foliar application was made before start of flowering, second at the time of fruit set and third application was repeated at 15

days after fruit set. They reported that the tallest plant height (77.22 to 88.14), maximum number of primary branches per plant (1.83 to 2.61) and number of secondary branches per plant (4.47 to 7.44) were recorded in the treatment which received in boron concentration at the rate of 0 to 0.25 % but adding more boron concentration at the rate of 0.5 %, will decreased the plant height/number of primary branches per plant/number of secondary branches of tomato. Moreover, the plant height, number of primary branches per plant and number of secondary branches per plant (86.53, 2.53 and 6.42 respectively) were increased consistently with increasing concentration of zinc as foliar spray at the rate of 0.5 %.

An experiment conducted by Rahman *et al.* (2019) on BARI on tomato revealed that the different levels of zinc exhibited significant effect on total soluble solids, Beta carotene and vitamin C content of tomato fruits. The maximum TSS content, beta carotene and vitamin C of fruits was found from zinc at the rate of 0.5 kg/ha. Minimum TSS content was obtained from zinc at the rate of 1 kg/ha. The beta carotene and vitamin C were the lowest in control. The result of an experiment on tomato conducted by Ullah *et al.* (2019) revealed that the different levels of boron (B1: 0 kg/ha, B2: 1 kg/ha, B3: 2 kg/ha) significantly influenced the yield of fruits per hectare. The highest yield (77.2 t/ha) was produced due to the application of 2 kg of boron. On the other hand, the lowest yield (49.0 t/ha) was produced in control treatment and also showed that application of boron gave higher yield per hectare than untreated control in tomato.

b) Brinjal

Zinc deficiency symptoms in Brinjal

Zinc deficiency inhibits both vegetative growth and fruit production. It causes shortening of internodes, appears in acidic soils and most of them found in sandy, calcareous soil. Delayed flowering and the flowers fails to set fruits and withered.

Boron deficiency symptoms in Brinjal

In brinjal, the distal ends of the young, fully developed leaves become yellow. Midribs, veins, and mesophyll show the symptoms, i.e., interveinal chlorosis on the entire leaf. It was suggested that the symptoms were due to boron (B) deficiency although B supply was assumed to be sufficient.

Suganiya *et al.* (2015) conducted an experiment at crop farm of Eastern university of Sri Lanka on brinjal cv. Thirunellveli purple. The treatments comprised of 0 ppm, 50 ppm and 150 ppm of Boron in plants, sprayed 3 times first at full bloom

and other 2 spray were given at 10 days interval. The maximum number of flower buds/plant, number of flower/axil, total number of flower cluster/plant and number of flower/plant were recorded with the application of 150 ppm of boron and minimum flowering characters were observed in control treatment.

Saleha *et al.* (2015) reported that application of FYM at the rate of 25 tones/ha along with RDF (100:50:50 kg/ha) in soil plus 0.2 % zinc as foliar spray after 40 days of transplanting had recorded that the highest number of leaves per plant in brinjal. According to the results of an experiment conducted by Mahesh *et al.* (2017) on brinjal the treatments which received 10 mg Zn + 10 mg B had recorded the maximum number of flowers per plant (18.32) and minimum number of flower was found in control (6.56) at 60 days after transplanting.

In Brinjal, a study conducted by Uikey *et al.* (2018) on Utkarsha F1 hybrid suggested that the foliar application of micronutrients significantly influenced the growth parameters. The maximum plant height and number of leaves per plant and number of branches per plant was found in the RDF + Borax (0.2 %) + $FeSO_4$ (0.5 %) + $ZnSO_4$ (0.5 %), (82.67 cm, 173.27 and 12.60 respectively), which was followed by RDF + Borax (0.2 %) + $ZnSO_4$ (0.5 %) which recorded the next best value of plant height and number of leaves per plant and number of branches per plant (80.61 cm, 170.80 and 12.20 respectively). However, minimum growth parameter was observed in control.

An investigation carried out by Mahesh *et al.* (2019) on brinjal cv. Rutika showed a significant positive response for different levels of zinc and boron. At 90 days after transplanting, maximum fruit yield per plant was found in 10 mg Zn + 10 mg B (919 g). The minimum yield was found in control (384 g/plant).

c) Chilli and Capsicum

Boron deficiency symptoms in chilli

Deficiency causes stunted growth in chilli plants and is characterized by interveinal chlorosis, or the yellowing of leaves and leaf veins remain green. The boron-deficient plants usually exhibit two key visible symptoms: depression of growing points (root tip, bud, flower, and young leaf) and deformity of organs (root, shoot, leaf, and fruit).

Zinc deficiency symptom in chilli

It is important in the production of chlorophyll, the absorption of water and the growth of leaf and stem. Plants that are zinc deficient will display yellow or grey

patches between the veins of new growth. The end leaves may form a rosette or appear narrow and distorted.

In green chilli, a study undertaken by Datir *et al.* (2012) showed that number of branches varied significantly for soil application of different zinc levels at the rate of 0, 2.5 and 5 kg/ha at 40 and 60 days after transplanting. The highest number of branches was observed from 2.5 kg/ha, followed by 5 kg/ha of zinc/ha and minimum number of leaves was recorded from control treatment. Rafique *et al.* (2012) conducted an experiment on the effect of boron fertilization on dry fruit yield of chilli cultivars Nepali, ICPN 15 #4 and loungi. The results showed that the application of boron at the rate of 2kg/ha increased the dry fruit yield significantly in the loungi variety.

Angami *et al.* (2017) conducted a study on chilli variety 'kasha Anmol' and revealed a significant increase in quantity of beta carotene (4.98 mg/100 g) from $ZnSO_4$ 0.2 %, followed by the treatment $ZnSO_4$ 0.4 % (4.83 mg/100 g), while minimum value of beta carotene (2.38) was found in control. Highest capsaicin, the phenolic pungent principal (0.69 %) of chilli, was obtained in the $MnSO_4$ 0.4 % and minimum value of capsaicin (0.26) was found in control.

In an experiment on chilli, Harris *et al.* (2018) found that the different concentrations of boron and magnesium has significantly influenced the number of branches and number of leaves per plant. The maximum number of branches and number of leaves per plant (17 and 27) were recorded in the treatment B150 ppm + Mg 150 ppm, applied as foliar spray, the first application was done at flower bud initiation stages and second spray at 14 days after the first spray. While minimum number of branches and number of leaves per plant (10 and 15) were recorded in control.

An investigation carried out by Ramgiry *et al.* (2019) on chilli reported that the maximum value of seed yield (3.93q/ha) was observed from $FeSo_4$ (0.2 %) + boron (0.1 %) and followed by the treatment $FeSO_4$ (0.2 %) + Ca $(NO_3)_2$ (0.2 %) which registered 3.64 q/ha. The minimum seed yield (1.97 q/ha) was recorded in the treatment which received Ca $(NO_3)_2$ (0.2 %) at 3 days after transplanting.

A research work conducted by Ashruf *et al.* (2020) on chilli revealed that the tallest plant height (76.18 cm) was recorded in the treatment which received $ZnSO_4$ +B_2O_3 (1.0 + 0.8 g) applied as foliar spray starting from 45 days after transplanting at 20 days interval. The maximum fruit length (12.49 cm), maximum pedicel length (3.17 cm) was found in the treatment $ZnSO_4$ + B_2O_3 (0.75 + 0.6 g), while treatment

control produced minimum fruit length of 7.82 cm. The minimum level of pedicel length (2.83 cm) was observed from control treatment.

d) Potato

Boron deficiency symptoms in Potato

Symptoms of boron deficiency in potatoes are seen on the shoot, although reduced growth with short internodes and curled leaves have been reported, more readily seen in the tubers in the form of brown necrotic patches.

Zinc deficiency symptoms in Potato

Leaves are smaller and growth is stunted. The leaves are deformed and folded inwards ('fern leaf of potato'). Mature leaves are affected mostly greyish brown to bronze coloured blotches appear first on the middle of the leaves, later all over the foliage, Leaf blades show interveinal chlorosis.

In potato, a study conducted by Banerjee *et al.* (2017) reported that the maximum potato starch content was recorded with RDF+ 6.0 kg of zinc/ha applied at 30 days after planting. This was followed by the treatment RDF+ 4.5 kg of zinc/ha and minimum potato starch content was found in RDF+ 1.5 kg of zinc/ha with RDF (200:150:150 kg/ha). An experiment carried out by Muthanna *et al.* (2017) in potato variety Kufri Lalima at Horticulture Research Farm Bangladesh, Hindu University, Varanasi, revealed that the maximum number of sprouts per tuber (6.67) at 40 days after planting was found in treatment RDF + 2 kg B. The minimum number of sprouts per tuber (3.33) was recorded in the treatment which received RDF + 2 kg B + 30 kg S and RDF + 2 kg B.

Mumtak *et al.* (2019) reported that the maximum average weight of tuber of 127 g was recorded in the treatment which received FYM (25 t/ha) + RDF (150:120:100 kg NPK/ha + 0.1 % Borax + 0.2 % $ZnSO_4$ + 0.2 % $MnSO_4$). The first foliar spray of micronutrient was applied at plant establishing stage, second at tuber initiation stage and third spray was done at tuber bulking stag. The minimum value of average weight of tuber 118 g was found in control treatment. Sarkar *et al.* (2019) suggested that the boron uptake increased significantly as boron application is increased. The uptake of boron was the highest in the treatment which received RDF + 0.1 % boric acid as foliar application at 40, 50, and 60 DAP.

The results of an experiment conducted by Lenka *et al.* (2020) suggested that the boron and zinc application significantly increased the tuber bulking rate in potato. The treatment which received 200:150:150 kg of NPK/ha + foliar spray of 0.1 % zinc (zinc sulphate) + 0.1 % boron (boric acid) at 40, 50 and 60 DAP) had

recorded the maximum tuber bulking rate at 50 to 65 DAP (20.15 gm/days) and 65 to 80 DAP (9.48 gm/day). The minimum tuber bulking rate 17.60 and 8.64 gm/day at 50 to 65 DAP and 65 to 80 DAP respectively was recorded in the treatment RDF (200:150:150 kg of NPK /ha).

7. Conclusion

Micronutrients play an indispensable role in growth and development of vegetable crops. The nutritional value of crops is becoming a major issue, therefore, application of boron and zinc micronutrients to sustain soil health and crop productivity besides maintaining the quality of vegetables is profound importance. And this micronutrients are beneficial for improve yield, quality, earliness, fruit setting and increases in shelf life of vegetable crops.

8. References:

1) Alia, M. H., Mehrajb, H and Jamal Uddin, A. F. M. 2015. Effect of foliar application of zinc and boron on growth and yield of summer tomato. *J. Biosci. Agric. Res.* 6(1): 512 - 517.

2) Angami, T., Chandra, A., Makdoh, B., Raghav, C.S., Assumi, S.R., Baruah, S., Bam, B., Sen, A and Kalita, H. 2017. Promising influence of micronutrient on yield and quality of chilli under mid hill conditions under and boron nutrition in entisols of India. *Int. J. Life Sci.,* 12(3): 1633-1636.

3) Ashraf, M.I., Liaqat, B., Anam, L., Kiran, S., Asghar, R., Shaukat, M.B. and Hussain, N. 2020. Effect of foliar application of zinc and boron on growth and yield of chilli (*Capsicum frutescens* L.). *Int. J. Agron. Agric. Res.* 16(3): 12 - 18.

4) Banerjee, H., Sarkar, S., Deb, P., Chakraborty, I., Sau, S. and Ray, K. 2017. Zinc fertilization in potato: a physiological and bio-chemical study. *Int. J. Plant & Soil Sci.* 16(2): 1-13.

5) Gurumani, A.R., Jalal, U.D., Sami, U.K., Rani, A., Kashik, W., Ahmed, K., and Hadyatullah. 2012. Soil application of improves growth and yield of tomato. *Int. J. Agric. Biol.* 14(1): 91-96.

6) Haleema, B., Rab, A., Hussain, S.A. 2018. Effect of calcium, boron and zinc foliar application on growth and fruit production of tomato. *Sarhad J. of Agric.* 34(1): 19-30.

7) Harris, K.D., Vanajah, T. and Puvanitha, S. 2018. Effect of foliar application of boron and magnesium on growth and yield of green chilli (*Capsicum annum* L.). *J. Agric. Sci.* 12(1): 26 - 49.

8) Jeanine, M.D., Sanders, D.C., Nelson, P.V., Lengnick, L and Sperry, W. J. 2003. Boron improves growth, yield, quality, and nutrient content of tomato. *J. Amer. Soc. Hort. Sci.* 128(3): 441-446.

9) Lenka, B., Divya, R.K. and Das, S.K. 2020. Nutrient use effeciency, yield attributes and comparative economics of potato crop (*Solanum tuberosum* L.) in response to zinc and boron nutrition in entisols of India. *Int. J. Chem. Stud.* 8(3): 10-17.

10) Mahesh, M.S., John, S.A., Telangre, S.S. and Ingole, D.D. 2020. Effect of zinc and boron on quality of brinjal fruits (*Solanum melongena* L.). *Int. J. Chem. Stud.* 8(1): 1915-1918.

11) Mahesh, M.S., Solanki, M.S., Thakare, G., Jogi, P.D. and Sapkal, D.R. 2017. Effect of zinc and boron on growth of brinjal (*Solanum melongena* L.). *Int. J. Plant Sci.* 12(2): 160-163.

12) Meena, D.C., Maij, S., Meena, J.K., Govind, Kumawat, R., Meena, K.R., Kumar, S., and Sodh, K. 2015. Improvement of growth, yield and quality of tomato (*Solanum lycopersicum* L.) cv. Azard T-6 with foliar application of zinc and boron. *Int. J. Stress Mgt.* 6(5): 598-601.

13) Miyu, M., Sarma, P., Warade, S., Hazarika, B., Debnath, P., Ramjan, M. and Ansari, M.T. 2019. Effect of foliar application of micronutrients on potato (*Solanum tuberosum* L.) cv. "Kufri Joyti" for growth, yield & quality attributes. *Int. J. Chem. Stud.* 7(3): 4813 - 4817.

14) Muthanna, M. A., Singh, A.K., Tiwari, A., Jain, V.K. and Padhi, M. 2017. Effect of boron and sulphur application on plant growth and yield attributes of potato (*Solanum tuberosum* L.). *Int. J. Curr. Microbiol. App. Sci.* 6(10): 399-404.

15) Naz, R.M.M., Muhammad, S., Hamid, A. and Bibi, F. 2012. Effect of boron on the flowering and fruiting of tomato. *Sarhad J. Agric.* 28(1): 37-40.

16) Osman, I.M., Hussein, M.H., Ali, M.T., Mohamed, S.S., Kabir, M.A., Halder, B.C. 2019. Effect of boron and zinc on the growth, yield and yield contributing traits of tomato. *J. Agri. Veterinary Sci.* 12(2): 25-37.

17) Rafique, E., Hassan, M.M., Khokhar, K.M., Ishaq, M., Yousra, M. and Tabassam, T. 2012. Boron requirement of chili (*Capsicum annuum* L.): proposed diagnostic criteria. *J. Plant Nutr.* 35(5): 739-749.

18) Rahman, M.D., Saki, M.D.S., Hosai, M.D.T., Rashid, S. 2019. Cumulative effect of zinc and gibberellic acid on yield and quality of tomato. *Int. J. Biosci.* 14(3): 350-360.

19) Ramgiry, M., Ramgiry, P. and Verma, B.K. 2019. Effect of foliar spray of micronutrients to enhance seed yield and quality in chilli (*Capsicum annuum* L.). *Int. J. Pure App. Biosci.* 7(2): 275-278.

20) Rafique, E., Mahmood, U.H.M., Khohar, K.M., Ishaq, M., yousra, M., and Tabassam, T. (2012). Boron requirement of chilli (*Capsicum annum* L.). *J. Plant. Nutr.* 35(5): 739-749.

21) Sarkar, S., Banerjee, H. and Dutta, S. 2018. Influence of boron on productivity, profitability and quality of processing-grade potato. *J. Environ. Biol.* 39: 1-10.

22) Suganiya, S.A., Kumuthini and Harrisb, D. 2015. Effect of boron on flower and fruit set and yield of ratoon brinjal crop. *Int. J. Sci. Res. Innova. Technol.* 2(1): 135-141.

23) Tawab, S., Gohar, A., Faiza, T., Owais, K., Nadia, B., Ghazala, R., Shawana, A., and Ume, K.A. (2015). Response of brinjal (*Solanum melongena* L.) cultivars to zinc levels. *J. Agric. Biol Sci.* 10(5): 172-178.

24) Uikey, S., Das, M., Ramgiry, P.P., Vijayvergiya, D., Ghaday, P., Ali, S.A. and Pradhan, J. 2018. Effect of zinc, boron and iron on growth and phenological characters of brinjal (*Solanum melongena* L.). *Int. J. Curr. Microbiol. App. Sci.* 7(9): 1643-1649.

Scientific Advancements in Current Agricultural Research
ISBN: 978-81-947154-7-4
First Edition; 2020
Chapter – 4, Page: 39 - 54

4

MYCORRHIZAE IN VEGETABLE CROPS

S. Kamalakannan*, T. Soniya, T. Uma Maheswari, S. Kumar and R. Sudhagar

Department of Horticulture, Faculty of Agriculture, Annamalai University, Annamalai Nagar,
Tamil Nadu, India.
*Corresponding author: kamalhort@gmail.com

Abstract

Mycorrhizae are beneficial fungi and nearly all plant species are associated with mycorrhizal symbionts. Mycorrhizal fungi are ubiquitous in soils and make up between 5 – 36 % of the total biomass of the soil and between 9 – 55 % of the biomass of microorganisms in the soil. It is mainly used as a biofertilizer, biocontrol for bioremediation, soil conservation and photostimulation. In plants, mycorrhiza increases the surface area of roots for improved uptake of water and nutrients. AM fungi hydrolyses organic phosphates present in soil and provide soluble phosphates to their host plant. In soil with low phosphate content, mycorrhizae also help plants absorb copper and zinc by similar mechanism.

Key words: Mycorrhizae, Biofertilizer, Biocontrol, Phosphate solubilization and Vegetable crops.

1. Introduction

Mycorrhizal fungi are beneficial fungi that are associated with plant roots *via* a symbiotic association whereby both the host plant and the fungus benefit (Frank, 1885). The term Mycorrhizae is derived from the Greek word "mycos", meaning fungus, and "rhiza", meaning root (Parniske,2008). Two major types of mycorrhizae are known: ecto and endomycorrhizae. The ectomycorrhizae are characterized by an

extracellular fungal growth in the root cortex while the endomycorrhizae are characterized by forming inter and intracellular fungal structures called as vesicles and arbuscles (Dar and Reshi, 2017). Nearly all plant species are associated with mycorrhizal symbionts. Because of their importance to plants and their widespread distribution, mycorrhizae must be considered in all aspects of plant ecology, crop science, and agriculture. Mycorrhizal fungi are divided into seven different types: ectomycorrhiza, vesicular arbuscular mycorrhiza (abbreviated as VA mycorrhiza), ectendomycorrhiza, arbutoid, monotropoid, ericaceous mycorrhiza, and orchidaceous mycorrhiza. Mycorrhizal fungi are ubiquitous in soils and make up between 5 – 36 % of the total biomass of the soil and between 9 – 55 % of the biomass of microorganisms in the soil (Goltapeh *et al.*, 2008). Among the various mycorrhizae, endomycorrhizae and ectomycorrhizae are the most abundant and widespread (Jagnaseni *et al.*, 2016). Mycorrhizal association can be either intracellular, as in Arbuscular Mycorrhizal Fungi (AMF), or extracellular as in ectomycorrhizal fungi. They are an important component of soil fertility. It is mainly used as a biofertilizer, biocontrol for bioremediation, soil conservation and photostimulation. This chapter deals in detail about the use of AM fungi in various vegetable crops and their role in enhancing the growth and yield of vegetables.

2. AM Fungi association with Plants

AM fungi are commonly associated with agricultural, horticulture crops in addition to tropical trees. Paleobotanical and molecular sequence data suggest that the first land plants formed associations with Glomalean fungi from the Glomeromycota about 460 million years ago. This is estimated to be some 300–400 million years before the appearance of root nodule symbiosis with nitrogen-fixing bacteria (Finlay, 2008). These fungi are also referred to as biotrophic symbionts that are unable to exist without their plant partner and cannot be artificially cultivated *in vitro* (Kavkova, 2014). About 150 species in the only six genera which are able to form AM (*Acuulospora, Entrophospora, Gigaspora, Glomus, Sclerocystis and Scutellospora*) have been systematized; none of these fungi have yet been successfully cultured axenically (Aguilar and Barea, 1995). AM fungi are able to create a symbiosis with most vegetables including major crops of different families, such as: Alliaceae, Apiaceae, Asteraceae, Fabaceae and Solanaceae (Baum *et al.*, 2015).

- *Arbuscules* – AM fungi form a shrub-shaped structure inside the root cortical cells by branching in several very thin hyphae. This is where the exchange of nutrients and carbon happens between the host plant and the fungus (Berruti *et al.*, 2014).

- *Vesicles* - These are spherical or oval bodies with a thin wall, and contain lipid cells which in terms of swollen chain endsor some of its middle parts, are created inside or between root's skin cells, and in the case of intercellular they are confined with plasma membrane similar to Arbuscule. These organs are only formed in fungal species belonging to the Order of the *Glomineae*. These store the stock for both the fungi and the plant (Alizadeh, 2011).
- *Hyphae* – It is a root-like structure that grow outside the root, in long distances to explore the soil for nutrients. AM fungi form hyphal networks that can contain over 100 meters of hyphae per cubic centimeter of soil, and are important for nutrient uptake and soil aggregation (Parniske, 2008).
- *Spores* – Most AM fungi will propagate from spores in the soil. Some genera, like members of the *Glomus* genus, can also propagate from broken hyphae segments (Troeh and Loynachan, 2009).

After the formation of these organs, they do not go away and they last till the end of fungus life time. The relationship between fungi and plants is peaceful, because on one side fungus provides the plants with nourishment, and on the other side it receives the necessary carbohydrates and energy from the host plant.

In plants, mycorrhiza increases the surface area of roots for improved uptake of water and nutrients. Immobile nutrients are absorbed by plants through diffusion. In nutrient depleted, tropical regions with excessive rainfall where essential nutrients are leached from soil surfaces, mycorrhizal fungi can extend their external hyphae beyond the depleted zones. Phosphorus is an extremely immobile element present in the soil. The major role of VA is to supply phosphorus to plant roots. AM fungi hydrolyses organic phosphates present in soil and provide soluble phosphates to their host plant. In soil with low phosphate content, mycorrhizae also help plants absorb copper and zinc by similar mechanism. Arbuscular mycorrhizae fungi expand the rhizosperic exploratory area of plant root system through their ramifying hyphae and help in acquisition of nutrients especially phosphorus and soil moisture. Thus, enhanced Phosphorus supply and plant water relations in mycorrhizae plants may lead to better fruiting behavior and productivity in crops (Auge, 2006). Nitrogen is present in soil in the form of ammonium and nitrate. Ammonium, nitrate and amino acids are absorbed by the extra radical mycelium of fungi. The hyphae of arbuscular mycorrhizae fungi produce the glycoprotein glomin, which may be one of the major stores of carbon in the soil.

3. Effect of Mycorrhizae on Growth attributes

A field experiment was conducted at Annamalai University, Tamil Nadu to study the influence of different vesicular arbuscular mycorrhizal fungi *viz., Glomus fasciculatum, G. mossae* and *Giagaspora margarita.* The results revealed that maximum shoot length, number of leaves and leaf area were recorded in the treatment which received NPK plus *Giagspora margarita* (Kamalakannan and Manivannan, 2002).

In pepper (*Capsicum annuum* L.) variety Cacho de cabra Castillo *et al.* (2009) found that the mycorrhizal inoculation increased the growth rate of the plant measured as height, which in the *G. claroideum* treatment increased rapidly until 90 DAS. Significant differences were found at 216 DAS in the measurements between *G. claroideum* and without inoculation control. The *G. claroideum* treatment had registered the greatest height, with an average of 66.5 cm, 15.2 % higher than *G. intraradices* (57.7 cm) and 30.8 % higher than the control (50.8 cm).

A research work conducted in the greenhouse of the Horticulture Department, Faculty of Agriculture, Luyengo Campus, University of Swaziland, by Oseni *et al.* (2010) in tomato seeds *Lycopersicon esculentum* L. var. rodade reported that AM fungi (strain - Biocult) inoculated seedlings exhibited better transplant performance due to its higher fresh root weight (avg. 2.17 g plant^{-1}), high shoot/root ratio (avg. 0.236) and higher fresh root biomass (avg.11.28 g plant^{-1}).

The effects of indigenous *Glomus* sp. and Bioorganics (*Glomus aggregatum, G. clarum, G. deserticola, G. intraradices, G. monosporus, G. mosseae, Gigaspora margarita,* and *Paraglomus brasilianum*) on tomato, pepper, and cucumber plant development were evaluated by Yildiz (2010) in Turkey. He observed that the indigenous *Glomus* sp. showed positive effects on cucumber and tomato plant growth, but there was no significant difference in pepper plant growth when compared with the Bio Organics treatments. *Glomus* sp. colonization rates on roots of plants were 71 % in cucumber, 72 % in tomato, and 61 % in pepper, and Bio Organics colonization rates were 47 % in cucumber, 39 % in tomato, and 36 % in pepper.

At Argentina, in pepper, Beltrano *et al.* (2013) found that leaf area was higher at high P level than at low P level in both mycorrhizal inoculated and non-mycorrhizal plants and decreased with salinity stress. The maximum leaf area was recorded in the treatment which received mycorrhizal inoculation plus 40 mg kg^{-1} phosphorus plus zero salinity level. Under high phosphorus levels, the leaf area decreased in the mycorrhizal inoculated plants as the salinity level increased to 200 mM. The maximum chlorophyll content (1.57 mg 100^{-1}) was recorded in the treatment which received mycorrhizal inoculation plus 10 mg kg^{-1}phosphorus plus

Chapter - 4

zero salinity level. Mycorrhizal colonisation improved the chlorophyll content under moderate (100 mM NaCl) and severe (200 mM NaCl) stress conditions, compared with non-mycorrhizal plants, but did not modify the chlorophyll content under non-stressed (0 mM NaCl) or low stressed (50 mM NaCl) conditions.

The growth of three local varieties of Okra, *viz.,* Parbhanikranti, Arkaanamica and Selection-51 were assessed by Darade (2015) with inoculation of VAM fungi (100 gm/pot) such as *Glomus fasciculatum* and *Gigaspora gigantea* at nursery stage by pot culture experiment at Department of Botany, Govt. Vidarbha Institute of Science and Humanities, Amravati, Maharastra. After 70 DAS, Increase in biomass was recorded in plants inoculated with VAM fungi as compared to uninoculated plants. The cultivar Parbhanikranti was found highly susceptible to *Glomus fasciculatum* shows maximum response in growth parameters like, increase in number of leaves, flowers and fruit set, while minimum growth response was recorded in Selection – 51. Of the two Vesicular Arbuscular Mycorrhizal Fungi, *Glomus fasciculatum* was found most effective in growth of plant as compared to *Gigaspora sgigantea*.

A study conducted by Bai *et al.* (2016) at Department of Soil Science, CSK, Himachal Pradesh Agricultural University, Palampur, Himachal Pradesh, India in garden pea suggested that at 60 days after sowing, both maximum plant height and leaf area index was registered in Arbuscular mycorrhizal fungi + *Rhizobium* + $N_{100\%}$ $P_{100\%}$, which was significantly higher over 100 % NPK + 14.5 t FYM ha^{-1} (Generalized recommended dose) by about 24.3 %. At 120 DAS, treatment-wise trend with reference to plant height and leaf area index was similar to that obtained during 60 DAS with taller plants in dual-inoculated treatments.

In an experiment on orka-pea cropping system at CSK Himachal Pradesh Agricultural University, Palampur Kumar *et al.* (2016) reported that the AMF inoculation significantly improved the root colonization in okra from 7 – 29 %. Further, root colonization was high at low levels of applied-P while it decreased with increasing P. In pea, AMF showed higher root colonization at 50 % P, while it decreased at higher applied-P (75 to 100 %) at either of two irrigation regimes. Overall, AMF enhanced the extent of root colonization by 2 to 2.3 fold than non-AMF treatments.

At College of Horticultural Science, Henan Agricultural University, Zhengzhou, China, Chen *et al.* (2017) conducted an experiment in Cucumber seed (*Cucumis sativus* L. cv. Zhongnong No. 106), and suggested that the growth of cucumber seedlings was significantly improved by inoculation with AMF. For instance, compared to the control, VT (*Claroideoglomus* sp., *Funneliformis* sp.,

Chapter - 4

Diversispora sp., *Glomus* sp., and *Rhizophagus* sp.) inoculation increased dry weight of shoot, dry weight of root and root to shoot ratio by 72.15, 112.94, and 23.72 %, respectively, while Fm (*Funneli formismosseae*) inoculation increased those by 27.24, 58.22, and 24.51%, respectively, implying that AMF-induced growth increment was predominantly attributed to root as compared to shoot. Moreover, the infection rates of cucumber seedlings inoculated with VT, BF (*Glomus intraradices, G. microageregatum* BEG and *G. claroideum* BEG 210) and Fm were 82.38, 74.65, and 70.32 % on day 46 after inoculation.

In a greenhouse experiment on tomato carried out at Department of Plant Pathology, College of Agriculture, University of Sargodha, Pakistan, Khan *et al.* (2017) reported that both higher shoot weight and shoot length was recorded in MF (200 g/pot) + Healthy treatment (21.10 g and 29.13 cm) as compared to other treatments. This was followed by MF (200 g/pot) + *M. incognita* combined treatment (19.91 g and 27.60 cm).

The results of an experiment conducted by Nasir *et al.* (2018) at USDA-ARS, Eastern Regional Research Center, Molecular Characterization of Food borne Pathogens Research Unit, Wyndmoor, PA 19038, USA suggested that AM fungi inoculations on garden leek plants at seedling stage resulted in significant differences in the plant height of garden leeks when compared to the non-inoculated (control) plants. The average plant height generally ranged from 17.8 cm in leeks inoculated with *G. geosporum* to 25 cm in plants inoculated with *R. intraradices*. The mean height of the un-inoculated (control) plants was 18 cm. The height of garden leek plants inoculated with *G. geosporum*, *C. claroideum*, and *Glomus* sp. did not differ significantly from the non-mycorrhizae control garden leeks. The root colonization of garden leek plants differed significantly among the AM fungal species. Root colonization of all inoculated treatments also differed significantly from the non- mycorrhizal control plants. The percentage of root colonization in garden leeks ranged from 0 (no colonization in non-mycorrhizae control) to 72 % in plants inoculated with *R. intraradices*.

A research work carried out on a farmer's field at Keela Thanneerpalli village, Kulithalai block, Karur district, Tamil Nadu during the year 2018. The treatments comprise of different combinations of Farm Yard Manure (FYM), recommended dose of fertilizers (RDF), zinc sulphate ($ZnSO_4$), Zinc Solubilising Bacteria (ZSB) and Vesicular Arbuscular Mycorrhizae (VAM). The results revealed that the maximum values for the growth attributes *viz.*, plant height (87.95 and 87.12 cm), number of branches (4.63 and 4.53), number of leaves (24.02 and 24.60), leaf area (220.36 and 190.51 cm_2) and dry matter production (140.10 and 138.41 g plant^{-1}) and

Chapter - 4

minimum intermodal length (4.33 and 4.37 cm) were recorded in the plots which received the application of FYM + RDF + ZSB + VAM + 40 kg ZnSO$_4$ ha^{-1} during the first and second season respectively. This treatment was closely followed by the treatment combination FYM + RDF + ZSB + VAM + 30 kg ZnSO$_4$, ha^{-1} and found to be on par with the best treatment (Kamalakannan *et al.*, 2019).

At Rani Durgawati University, Jabalpur Verma *et al.* (2019) conducted an experiment with nine vegetables of four family namely as Amaranthaceae, Cucurbitaceac, Poaceae and Solanaceae for maximum colonization of Arbuscular Mycorrhizal (AM) fungi. The highest rate of colonization was observed in *Solanum melongena* belonging to Solanaceae followed by *Solanum lycopersicum* (Solanaceae), and *Allium cepa* (Amaryllidaceae). The minimum colonization was observed in case of *Cucumis sativus* (Cucurbitaceae). The maximum average of colonization percentage was also recorded during the study and the highest frequency was showed in Solanaceae family about 93.47 % and minimum was found in Cucurbitaceae family about 66.7 %.

4. Effect of Mycorrhizae on Yield attributes

The results of an experiment conducted at Annamalai university, Tamil Nadu by Kamalakannan and Manivannan (2003) revealed that combination of 75 percent of nitrogen and phosphorus plus 100 percent potash plus Azospirillum plus G*igaspora margarita* had recorded the maximum shoot length, shoot weight and root yield. The results also indicated that inoculation of *Azospirillum* for fixing atmospheric nitrogen and VAM for mobilizing phosphorus reduced the 25 per cent of requirement of inorganic nitrogen and phosphorus fertilizers.

In potato, a study conducted by EL-Haddad and Awad (2007) during the two summer plantation of 2004 and 2005 at Abou Awad village, Aga, Dakahlia Governorate, Egypt reported that the interaction between NK rate, VAM fungi and micronutrient on potatoes yield and its components were significant on total tuber yield in both season and number of tuber/plant and tuber weight/plant in the first season only. The maximum total yield was obtained when potato plants were fertilized with 75 % NK, inoculated with VA mycorrhizae and foliar sprayed by micronutrient compared with untreated ones. The percentage increase in total tuber yield/fed was 19.72 % and 20.60 % in the first and second season, respectively.

In Turkey, at Department of Horticulture, Faculty of Agriculture University, Adana, Dasgan *et al.* (2008) conducted a study in greenhouse on tomato F$_1$M19 under hydroponic conditions and reported that fruit yield absolutely increased with AM inoculation in closed and open system. When compared with uninoculated

Chapter - 4

system, the total highest yield with 19.5 kg m^{-2} was produced with the treatment under open system with Mychorriza inoculation. The lowest yield was from the closed system without mychorriza treatment (16.8 kg m^{-2}).

In an experiment conducted at a farm in South-Eastern Pennsylvania, USA, Douds *et al.* (2015) found that the mean increase in yield of sweet potatoes of the AM inoculated plants for the experiment was statistically significant at 10.0±1.9 % over uninoculated control. Yield per plant ranged from a high of 3.8±0.08 (mean ± SEM) kg in 2009 to a low of 1.1 ± 0.1 kg for the short growing period in 2013. Though, the Mean Yield Range (MYR) was positive each year, and ranged from 19.2 % in 2009 to 7.1 % in 2014, yields were not significantly different for inoculated vs. uninoculated in any given year (eg. Pr>F =0.1817 for 2009). However, the mean MYR, 10.03 ± 1.86 %, was significantly different than zero (95 % CI: 5.25 % $\leq \bar{y} \leq$ 14.81 %), indicating a significant positive response over the long term. Further, roots collected at the time of harvest indicated significantly greater colonization by AM fungi of previously inoculated plants than in controls which became colonized by the indigenous population of AM fungi.

In common bean, Abdel-Fattah *et al.* (2016) reported that application of AMF 5 g/pot significantly increased the yield components of common beans with minimized levels of NPK compared to equivalent nonmycorrhizal ones. They further revealed that application of 75 % NPK with AMF had recorded the highest number of pods (21.66), length of pod (13.56 cm), pods weight (111.15 g), 100 seeds weight (9.36 g), weight of seed/plant (80.06 g), harvest index (1374.83) and intensity of mycorrhizal colonization (53.10 %). This was followed by fifty per cent NPK application with AMF.

In garden pea, Bai *et al.* (2016) observed the highest green pod yield with AMF *Rhizobium* (RHZ) $N_{100\%}P_{100\%}$ followed by AMF RHZ $N_{75\%}P_{75\%}$ and AMF RHZ $N_{50\%}P_{50\%}$, which exhibited significant respective increases of 25.5 %, 22.2 % and 12.3 % over NPK $_{100\%}$ FYM$_{14.5t}$ (Generalized recommended dose) The above treatments gave numerically higher, but non-significant increases of 3.8 % and 1.6 %, respectively, in pea pod yield over GRD. In AMF-imbedded treatments, magnitude of increase in the above parameter was to the tune of 6.6 % and 4.9 % in AMF $N_{100\%}P_{75\%}$ and $N_{100\%}P_{50\%}$ over GRD. The lowest pod yield was observed in absolute control followed by FP due to poor nutrition.

The experimental results conducted by Devhade *et al.* (2016) at Department of Seed Science and Technology, Faculty of Agriculture Bidhan Chandra Krishi Viswavidyalaya, Mohanpur, West Bengal in French bean revealed that pre-sowing

seed treatment of VAM @ 2 kg/ha had recorded more number of pods than the uninoculated treatments. Among the seven genotypes, fungi inoculated with VAM had recorded the maximum number of pods (38.70) and was followed by sonali (33.93). The minimum number pod was recorded in selection 9 (21.87). The results of an experiment carried out by Ahmed *et al.* (2017) in the greenhouse condition on Bottle gourd (*Lagenaria siceraria* (Mol.) Standl) during seasons of 2014/2015 and 2015/2016 at Central Laboratory for Agriculture Climate, Agricultural Research Centre, Dokki, Egypt, revealed that treating plants with mycorrhizae gave significant results in seed characteristics compared to untreated plants in both seasons. The interaction between mulching and mycorrhizae recorded very high values when compared with untreated plants. Black mulch plus mycorrhizae (BM_1) gave the highest value of seed weight/fruit (197.3 and 199.3 g) and seed yield/plant 828.7 and 857 g) compared to the control treatment which share the least significant level in both seasons, respectively.

An investigation carried out by Chandel *et al.* (2017) at Vegetable Research Farm, Department of Horticulture, Institute of Agricultural Sciences, BHU, Varanasi on tomato (*Solanum lycopersicum* L.) cv. Arka Vikas reported that soil application with Myc100 @ 250 g/ha has proven to be the best with respect to the characters *viz.*, number of fruits per plant (31.00), average fruit weight (91.95 g) and fruit yield per plant (2696.27 g). Untreated control has recorded the least values for the above said characters. The result of the experiment on garden peas conducted by Yadav *et al.* (2017) at CSK Himachal Pradesh Agricultural University, Palampur suggested that the integrated use of AM fungi and inorganic Phosphorus along with the irrigation regimes Irrigation water (mm)/cumulative pan evaporation (mm) 1.0 were recorded the maximum fresh pod weight of 4.1 g/pod at 120 DAS and yield of 9.87 t/ha. The next best value for yield was recorded which received Irrigation water (mm)/Cumulative pan evaporation (mm) 0.6 the lowest yield of 5.35 t/ha was recorded farmer practices as I_{WA} as per water availability.

In an experiment at Department of Agricultural Chemistry and Soil Science, at agricultural farm of Udai Pratap Autonomous College, Varanasi on onion, Kumar *et al.* (2018) found significant higher bulb diameter and yield with 100 % NPK + FYM @10 tons ha^{-1} + VAM @10 kg ha^{-1} in comparison to other treatments and followed by the treatment 150 % NPK + FYM @10 tons ha^{-1} + VAM @10 kg ha^{-1} were higher bulb diameter and yield were observed as (5.67 cm, 169.98 q/ha) respectively. The lowest bulb diameter and yield were showed in control. In okra, an experiment laid out in a farmer's field at Keela Thanneerpalli village, Kulithalai block, Karur district, Tamil Nadu by Kamalakannan *et al.* (2019a) revealed that the maximum values for the yield and its attributes *viz.*, number of fruits/plant (16.95

Chapter – 4

and 16.67), fruit length (11.96 and 11.90 cm), fruit grith (1.71 and 1.68 cm), single fruit weight (16.65 and 16.24 g), fruit yield (270.90 and 267.40 g/plant) and fruit yield/plot (26.41 and 25.40 kg) during first and second season, respectively) were recorded in the plots which received the application of FYM + RDF + Zinc Solubilizing Bacteria (ZSB) + Vesicular Arbuscular Mycorrhizae (VAM) + 40 kg $ZnSO_4$/ha. This treatment was closely followed by the treatment combination FYM + RDF + ZSB + VAM + 30 kg $ZnSO_4$/ha and found to be on par with the best treatment.

A field investigation in okra cv. Petra conducted by Al-Umrany *et al.* (2019) at Horticulture Department, College of Agriculture, Baghdad University, Al-Jadria, Iraq, recorded the highest yield at the $M_1F_2A_1$ (mycorrhizae @ 10 g. plant^{-1} + $FeSO_4$ @ 1g. L^{-1} + Anti-transpirant, 'Armurox' @5ml.L^{-1}) combination treatment with an average of 25.29 t/ha while the control treatment ($M_0F_0A_0$) gave the least amount of total yield (12.77 t/ha).

A research work was undertaken by Kamalakannan *et al.* (2019b) in the Department of Horticulture, Faculty of Agriculture, Annamalai University to find out the influence of biofertilizers and inorganic fertilizers on yield and root infection rate of VAM in radish. The treatments include 25, 50, 75 and 100 per cent of recommended dose of fertilizers along with *Azospirillum* and the VAM (*Giagaspora margarita*). The results of the experiment revealed that the combination of 75 per cent nitrogen and phosphorus plus 100 per cent potassium plus *Gigaspora margarita* had recorded the maximum yield of 33.03 tonnes per hectare. The maximum percentage of VAM infection in the roots of radish plants (63.33 per cent) was observed under the treatment which received 100 per cent nitrogen and potassium plus 25 per cent phosphorus plus VAM (*Gigaspora margarita*).

5. Effect of Mycorrhizae in Quality attributes

In radish, a study conducted by Kamalakannan and Manivannan (2008) found that the maximum ascorbic acid content (38 mg/100 g) was recorded in the treatment which involved NPK plus Phosphobacteria plus Glomusmossae. This was followed by the treatment NPK plus phosphobacteria plus *Glomus fasciculatum*. The fibre content was found to be minimum (0.8 %) in the treatment in which NPK plus *Azospirillum* plus *Gigaspora margarita* was applied.

A biochemical analysis on tomato fruits conducted by Chandrasekeran and Mahalingam (2015) at Department of Biology, Gandhi gram Rural Institute, Deemed University, Gandhigram, Dindigul, Tamil Nadu, India found that the tomato cultivated with AMF isolates increase the taste, colour, texture and chemical

composition. There were significant changes in the mean values between the analysed parameters. Glucose and fructose, lycopene and potassium concentrations were strongly and positively correlated, tomato fruit harvested from the treatment with *Glomus mosseae* (60 g/pot) showed the highest values for all the physicochemical parameters. Among all the AMF isolates *Glomus mosseae* treated tomato yields the best results followed by *Acaulospora* sp., *Glomus* sp., *Glomus aggregatum* and *Glomus fasiculatum.*

A study undertaken by Arif *et al.* (2018) at Department of Agricultural Chemistry, Bangladesh Agricultural University, Mymensingh, showed that in red amaranth (*Amaranthus tricolor*) maximum P, S, Mg, Fe and protein contents were observed due to the application of AMF and cow dung with phosphorus. The combined application of AMF with cow dung and phosphorus enhanced the association with plants and was more effective than only AMF application to enhance nutrient contents.

6. Effect of Mycorrhizae in Diseases protection

According to the results of an experiment conducted by Ali *et al.* (2018) in the net house and in the seed health laboratory, Department of Plant Pathology, Sher-e-Bangla Agricultural University, Dhaka during the period from May, 2015 to December, 2016, inoculation of pot grown vegetable plants with mycorrhizal plants resulted reduction in the incidence of diseases of vegetables. The damping off disease incidence was 10.78 %, 8.40 %, 10.05 %, 10.60 % and 7.60 % in non-inoculated Okra, Tomato, Brinjal, Chilli and Data respectively whereas in inoculated plant it was 4.52 %, 5.0 %, 2.0 %, 2.50 % and 5.0 % respectively. The result further showed that, in case of Root rot and Leaf spot the percentage of disease incidence was almost half in inoculated plants compared to non- inoculated plants.

7. Effect of Mycorrhizae on Nutrient uptake, Postharvest soil analysis and Economics

A field study was undertaken in the Department of Horticulture, Faculty of Agriculture, Annamalai University to find out the influence of biofertilizers and inorganic fertilizers on nutrient uptake in radish by Kamalakannan *et al.* (2019c). The treatments include 25, 50, 75 and 100 per cent of recommended dose of fertilizers along with *Azospirillum* and the VAM (*Gigaspora margarita*) in different combinations. The results of the experiment revealed that the combination of 75 per cent nitrogen and phosphorus and 100 per cent potassium plus *Azospirillum* plus VAM (*Gigaspora margarita*) had recorded the maximum nitrogen uptake of 49.72 kg ha^{-1}, phosphorus uptake of 17.93 kg ha^{-1} and potassium uptake of 59.43 kg ha^{-1}. This was followed by

the treatment which received 50 per cent nitrogen and phosphorus and 100 per cent potassium plus *Azospirillum* plus VAM (*Gigaspora margarita*).

An investigation carried out by Roshni *et al.* (2019) at Horticultural Research Station, Dr. Y. S. R. Horticultural University, Andhra Pradesh in Carrot seed cv. Pusa Rudhira suggested that different treatment combinations showed varying gross returns with respect to their input cost. The highest benefit cost ratio (3.04:1) was obtained in the treatment combination of 100 % RDF + PSB + KSB + *Azospirillum* + *Azotobacter* + VAM (F_1B_4) which recorded a gross return of Rs/ha 3,88,000, followed by the combination of 100 % RDF + PSB + KSB + *Azotobacter* (F_1B_2) with 2.87:1 which recorded a gross return of Rs/ha 3,64,888. The lowest benefit cost ratio (1.66:1) was recorded with the application of 75 % RDF + PSB + KSB+ VAM (F_2B_3) which yielded a gross return of Rs/ha 2,09,66. Kamalakannan *et al.* (2019d) reported that the combination of 100 per cent nitrogen, phosphorus and potassium plus *Azospirillum* plus VAM (*Gigaspora margarita*) had recorded the maximum available soil nitrogen of 185.18 kg ha^{-1}, phosphorus of 15.11 kg ha^{-1} and potassium of 284.79 kg ha^{-1}. The biofertilizers applied might have enriched the soil and hence the residual nitrogen, phosphorus and potassium left were higher.

8. Conclusion

The benefits of applying mycorrhizae to soil includes improvement in soil and plant ecosystem, increase in plant growth and establishment, reduction in transplanting stress and plant loss, improvement in soil structure and porosity, and reduction in the amount of chemical fertilizers requirement.

9. References

1) Abdel-Fattah, G. M., W. M. Shukry, M. M. B. Shokr and M. A. Ahmed. 2016. Application of mycorrhizal technology for improving yield production of common bean plants. International Journal of Applied Sciences and Biotechnology. 4(2): 191-197.
2) Ahmed, M. S., E. A. Salem and A. A. Helaly. 2017. Impact of Mycorrhizae and Polyethylene mulching on growth, yield and seed oil production of Bottle Gourd (*Lagenaria siceraria*). Journal of Horticultural Science & ornamental Plants. 9(1): 28-38.
3) Ali, M. M., M. N. H. Sani, M. Arifunnahar, F. M. Aminuzzaman, M. A. U. Mridha. 2018. Influence of arbuscular mycorrhizal fungi on growth, nutrient uptake and disease suppression of some selected vegetable crops. Azarian Journal of Agriculture. 5(6):190-196.

4) Alizadeh, O. (2011). Mycorrhizal Symbiosis. Advanced Studies in Biology, 3(6): 273-281.

5) Al-Umrany, H. H. A. and R. M. A. Al-obidy. 2019. The response of okra (*Abelmoschus esculentus* L. moench) to inoculation with the mycorrhizae and spray with FeSo₄ and anti-transpirant. Qadisiyah Journal for Agriculture Sciences, 9(1): 179 - 187.

6) Arif, T. U., A. Ghosh, S. G. Chamely, M. R. Haque and M. Rahman. 2018. Arbuscular mycorrhizal fungi inoculation with organic matter and phosphorus supplementation enhance nutrient contents of *Amaranthus tricolor* L. and *Basella alba* L. by improving nutrients uptake. The Journal of the Society for Tropical Plant Research, 5(3): 375-384.

7) Auge, R. M. 2006. Water relation, drought and VAM symbiosis. Mycorrhiza. 11: 3-42.

8) Azcon-Aguilar, C. and Barea, J.M., 1995. Saprophytic growth of arbuscular mycorrhizal fungi. In: A. Varma and B. Hock (Editors), Mycorrhiza Structure, Function, Molecular Biology and Biotechnology. Springer Verlag, Heidelberg, 391-407.

9) Bai, B., V. K. Suri, A. Kumar and A. K. Choudhary. 2016. Influence of dual inoculation of am fungi and *Rhizobium* on growth indices, production economics, and nutrient use efficiencies in Garden Pea (*Pisum sativum* L.). *Communications in Soil Science and Plant Analysis*, 47(8): 941 - 954.

10) Baum, C., W. EL-Tohamy, N. Gruda. 2015. Increasing the productivity and product quality of vegetable crops using arbuscular mycorrhizal fungi: A review. Scientia Horticulturae, 187: 131 - 141.

11) Beltrano, J., M. Ruscitti, M. C. Arango, and M. Ronco. 2013. Effects of arbuscular mycorrhiza inoculation on plant growth, biological and physiological parameters and mineral nutrition in pepper grown under different salinity and P levels. Journal of Soil Science and Plant Nutrition.13(1): 123-141.

12) Berruti, A., R. Borriello, A. Orgiazzi, A.C. Barbera, E. Lumini and V. Bianciotto. 2014. Arbuscular mycorrhizal fungi and their value for ecosystem management, biodiversity – The dynamic balance of the planet.

13) Castillo, C., L. Sotomayor, C. Ortiz, G. Leonelli, F. Borie and R. Rubio. 2009. Effect of arbuscular mycorrhizal fungi on an ecological crop of chilli peppers (*Capsicum annuum* L.). Chilean Journal of Agricultural Research, 69(1): 79-87.

14) Chandel, S. S., B. K. Singh, A. K. Singh, D. P. Moharana, A. Kumari and A. Kumar. 2017. Response of various mycorrhizal strains on tomato (*Solanum lycopersicum* L.) cv. Arka Vikas in relation to growth, yield, and quality attributes. Journal of Pharmacognosy and Phytochemistry, 6(6):2381-2384.

15) Chandrasekeran, A. and K. Mahalingam. 2015. Effect of arbuscular mycorrhizae fungi on the changes of physicochemical composition in tomato (*Lycopersicon esculentum*) fruit. Ecronicon Agriculture. 2(2): 317-324.

16) Chen , S., H. Zha, C. Zou, Y. Li, Y. Chen, Z. Wang, Y. Jiang, A. Liu, P. Zhao, M. Wang and G. J. Ahammed. 2017. Combined inoculation with multiple arbuscular mycorrhizal fungi improves growth, nutrient uptake and photosynthesis in cucumber seedlings. The Journal Frontiers in Microbiology. 8: 2516.

17) Dar, M. H. and Z. A. Reshi. 2017. Vesicular arbuscular mycorrhizal (VAM) fungi- as a major biocontrol agent in modern sustainable agriculture system. Russian Agricultural Sciences. 43(2): 138–143.

18) Darade, M. S. 2015. Effect of inoculation of VAM fungi on enhancement of biomass and yield in okra. International Journal of Innovative Science, Engineering & Technology. 2(8): 2348 - 7968.

19) Dasgan, H. Y., S. Kusvuran, and I. Ortas. 2008. Responses of soilless grown tomato plants to arbuscular mycorrhizal fungal (*Glomus fasciculatum*) colonization in re-cycling and open systems. African Journal of Biotechnology. 7(20): 3606-3613.

20) Devhade, P. G., N. Chamling and A. K. Basu. 2016. Variation in response of frenchbean genotypes towards pre-sowing seed treatment with VAM for seed yield. Journal of Crop and Weed. 12(1): 16-20.

21) Douds, D. D., J. Lee, J. E. Shenk and S. Ganser. 2015. Inoculation of sweet potatoes with AM fungi produced on-farm increases yield in high P soil. Journal of Applied Horticulture. 17(3): 171 - 175.

22) EL-Haddad, S. A. and EL. M. M. Awad. 2007. Influence of vesicular arbuscular mycorrhizae, NK fertilization rates and foliar application of micronutrients on growth, yield and quality of potatoes. Arab Univ. J. Agric. Sci., 15(2): 441-454.

23) Finlay, R. D. 2008. Ecological aspects of mycorrhizal symbiosis: with special emphasis on the functional diversity of interactions involving the extraradical mycelium. In Journal of Experimental Botany,59(5): 1115-1126.

24) Frank, A.B. 1885. On the nourishing, via root symbiosis, of certain trees by underground fungi, Reports of the German Botanical Society, 3: 128-145.

25) Goltapeh, E.M., Y.R. Danesh, R. Prasad and A. Varma. 2008. Mycorrhizal fungi: what we know and what we should know? In: Varma (editor). Mycorrhiza. Springer Verlag, Berlin.

26) Jagnaseni, B., A. Samanta, B. Saha and S. Datta. 2016. Mycorrhiza the oldest association between plant and fungi. Resonance, 1093-1104.

27) Kamalakannan, S. and K. Manivannan 2002. Influence of *Azospirillum*, phosphobacteria and vesicular arbuscular mycorrhizae on growth parameters of radish (*Raphanus sativus* L.). Res. on Crops, 3(1): 138 - 141.

28) Kamalakannan, S and K. Manivannan. 2003. Response of radish for graded levels of nitrogen and phosphorus along with biofertilizers. South Indian Hort., 51(1-6): 199 - 203.

29) Kamalakannan, S and K. Manivannan. 2008. Efficiency of VAM fungi along with *Azospirillum* and Phosphobacteria on the yield and quality of radish. Annamalai University Agric. J. (Golden Jubilee Special Issue), 23: 299 - 303.

30) Kamalakannan, S., R. Manikandan, K. Haripriya, R. Sudhagar and S. Kumar. 2019. Effect of zinc sulphate, zinc solubilizing bacteria and vesicular arbuscular mycorrhizae on growth attributes of okra. Plant Archives. 19(2): 3053 - 3056.

31) Kamalakannan, S., R. Manikandan, K. Haripriya, R. Sudhagar and S. Kumar. 2019a. Effect of zinc sulphate and biofertilizers on yield attributes and yield of okra [*Abelmoschus esculentus* (L.) Moench]. Res. on Crops. 20(4): 747 - 752.

32) Kamalakannan, S., K. Manivannan and R. Sudhagar. 2019b. Influence of biofertilizers and inorganic fertilizers on yield and root infection rate of VAM in radish. In: Abstracts of NLC India Limited and DST-PURSE Sponsored national conference on "Novel microbial technologies for sustainable agriculture and allied industries" (NMTSAAI – 2019) organized by Department of Agricultural Microbiology, Faculty of Agriculture, Annamalai University on 28th & 29th January, P – 55 – 56.

33) Kamalakannan, S., K. Manivannan and R. Sudhagar. 2019c. Nutrient uptake in radish as influenced by biofertilizers and inorganic fertilizers. In: Abstracts of UGC-SAP Sponsored National Seminar on "Advances In Plant Science Research (APSR - 2019)" organized by Department of Botany, Annamalai University, held on February 27-28, P – 57.

34) Kamalakannan, S., K. Manivannan and R. Sudhagar. 2019d. Influence of biofertilizers and inorganic fertilizers on post-harvest soil nutrient status in radish. In: Abstracts of DST-PURSE Sponsored national conference on "Climate resilient technologies for sustainable agriculture" (CRTSA-2019) organized by Department of Agronomy, Faculty of Agriculture, Annamalai University on 24th & 25th January, 2019, P – 168.

35) Kavkova, M. 2014. Mycorrhizal symbiosis. In Zahradnictvi, 33(3): 58–60.

36) Khan, A. R., W. Ashraf, W. A. Khan, H. Rehman, A. A. Khan and M. Mehdi. 2017. Role of *Glomus mosseae* and Neemexin the management of *Meloidogyne incognita* on tomato. Plant Protection, 01(02): 69 - 73.

37) Kumar, A., A. Singh, M. Kumar and A. K. Rai. 2018. Effect of integrated use of chemical fertilizers, fym and bio-fertilizers on crop productivity and soil fertility

under onion (*Allium cepa* L.). International Journal of Chemical Studies. 6(2): 3660 -3664.

38) Kumar, A., A. K. Choudhary and V. K. Suri. 2016. Influence of AM fungi and inorganic phosphorus on fruit and root characteristics, root colonization and soil phosphorus in okra- pea cropping system in Himalayan acid Alfisol. Indian Journal of Horticulture. 73(2): 213- 218.

39) Nasir, M. S. A., A. Nunez, L. C. McKeever and O. M. Olanya. 2018. Effects of arbuscular mycorrhizal fungal inoculations on the growth and polyphenol levels of garden leek (*Allium porrum*). Journal of Plant Protection Research. 58(1): 1427 - 4345.

40) Oseni, T. O., N. S. Shongwe and M. T. Masarirambi. 2010. Effect of Arbuscular mycorrhiza (AM) inoculation on the performance of tomato nursery seedlings in vermiculite. International Journal of Agriculture & Biology, 12: 789 – 792.

41) Parniske, M. 2008. Arbuscular mycorrhiza: the mother of plant root endosymbioses, Nature Rev. Microbiol., 6: 763 - 775.

42) Roshni, P., N. Murthy, K. U. Jyothi, S. Suneetha. 2019. Studies on influence of biofertilizers and NPK on nutrient uptake and production economics of carrot. International Journal of Chemical Studies. 7(3): 395 - 398.

43) Troeh, Z. I and T. E. Loynachan. 2009. Diversity of Arbuscular mycorrhizal fungal species in soils of cultivated soybean fields. Agron. J., 101: 1453 - 1462.

44) Verma, P., S. Barle, M. Shakya and S. S. Sandhu. 2019. Assessment of root colonization by VAM fungi in vegetable plants in central India. Global Journal of Bioscience and Biotechnology. 8(1): 60-66.

45) Yadav, A., V. K. Suri, A. Kumar and A. K. Choudhary. 2017. Effect of AM fungi and phosphorus   fertilization on P-use efficiency, nutrient acquisition and root morphology in pea (*Pisum sativum* L.) in an acid alfisol. Journal of Plant Nutrition. 10(3): 114 – 120.

46) Yildiz, A. 2010. A native *Glomus* sp. from fields in Aydın province and effects of native and commercial mycorrhizal fungi inoculants on the growth of some vegetables. Turk. J. Biol., 34: 447 - 452.

Scientific Advancements in Current Agricultural Research
ISBN: 978-81-947154-7-4
First Edition; 2020
Chapter – 5, Page: 55 - 63

5

WINE PRODUCTION FROM FRUITS

T. Uma Maheswari[1*], A. Rajavel[1], R. Sudhagar[1] and P. Sivasakthivelan[2]

[1]Department of Horticulture, Faculty of Agriculture, Annamalai University,
Annamalai Nagar, Tamil Nadu, India
[2]Department of Agricultural Microbiology, Faculty of Agriculture, Annamalai University,
Annamalai Nagar, Tamil Nadu, India

*Corresponding author: umahorti2003@gmail.com

Abstract

Wine is the alcoholic product obtained by fermentation of fruit juices with yeast. The following is the general procedure for the preparation of a fruit wine. Wines have been considered as safe and healthy drinks, besides an important adjunct to the diet. In wines, alcohol is a macro nutrient and is an energy source, capable of providing calories for all essential biological activities of the human cells, energy for physical work and thermo genesis. Wine making is one of the most ancient of man's technologies, and is now one of the most commercially prosperous biotechnological processes. Utilization of fruits in the production of fruit wines is a viable alternative that allows the use of harvest surpluses, results in the introduction of Value-added products into the market.

Keywords: Wine, Fruits, Fermentation, Alcoholic product and Value-added products.

1. Introduction

Wine is the alcoholic product obtained by fermentation of fruit juices with yeast as outlined by Joshi (1995). Wines have been considered as safe and healthy

drinks, besides an important adjunct to the diet. In wines, alcohol is a macro nutrient and is an energy source, capable of providing calories for all essential biological activities of the human cells, energy for physical work and thermo genesis (Bisson, 1995). It consists of water, alcohol, pigments, esters, vitamins, carbohydrates, minerals, acids, and tannins with medicinal and therapeutic value (Patil *et al.,* 2005). Fruit wines are produced and consumed in large quantities in all advanced countries in the world. A few industries in our country produce wine but fruit wine production at this time is insignificant in spite of tremendous increase in the fruit production (Joshi, 1995). Winemaking is one of the most ancient of man's technologies, and is now one of the most commercially prosperous biotechnological processes (Moreno-Arribas and Polo, 2005).

2. Grape wine

Padshetty *et al.* (1982) reported that the wines produced from grapes with yeast strain 101 fermented at a temperature of 15 °C recovered higher amount of ethyl alcohol and was adjudged better in quality. Suresh *et al.* (1985) found that four grape cultivars namely 'Arkavati', 'Arka Kanchan', 'Arka Shyam' and 'Arka Hans' were suitable for good quality dry wine production and the first three cultivars were suitable for good quality sweet wine production also. The effect of gibberllic acid treatment, method of juice extraction and pasteurization on quality of grape wine was studied by Ghadge (2006).

3. Jackfruit Wine

It is also possible to make wine using bulbs of jackfruit, according to the University of Agricultural Sciences, Gandhi Krishi Vignana Kendra, Bangalore, blending extracts of other fruits with "jackfruit wine" to increase the alcohol content either to the standards of "medium wine" or "heavy wine". It is because the team has found that only up to a maximum of seven per cent alcohol could be extracted from jackfruit. The study revealed that wine production from jackfruit juice by fermentation using *Saccharomyces cerevisiae* of *Baker* yeast was done in less than two weeks and is faster than that of natural fermentation (reported that the natural fermentation usually taken for 30 days). The jackfruit wine obtained was clear yellow in colour and brought strong jackfruit aroma (Kumoro *et al.,* 2012).

Jagtap *et al.* (2011) evaluated the antioxidant capacity of Jackfruit wine and its protective role against radiation induced DNA damage. Experimental results indicated that jackfruit wine was effective in DPPH radical scavenging (69.44 ± 0.34 %), FRAP (0.358 optical density value, O.D.), DMPD (78.45 ± 0.05%) and NO (62.46 ± 0.45 %) capacity. By the analysis of the High Performance Liquid

Chromatography coupled to diode array detector (HPLC-DAD), two phenolic compounds namely gallic acid and protocatechuic acid were identified. The jackfruit wine was also able to protect H_2O_2+UV radiation and γ-radiation (100 Gy) induced DNA damage in *pBR322* plasmid DNA. The antioxidant and DNA damage protecting properties of jackfruit wine confirmed health benefits when consumed and could become a valuable source of antioxidant rich neutraceuticals. Additionally, the wine could be a commercially valuable by-product for the jackfruit growers.

Matured well ripened jackfruit bulbs of Muttom Varikka variety were selected for the study. The study was conducted with five replications and four formulations in Completely Randomized Design varying only in sugar concentrations (T1: 50 %, T2: 45 %, T3: 40 %, T4: 35 %). Ten untrained panelists performed sensory evaluation test of the processed wine using 9 points hedonic scale. Among the treatments, T4 with 35 % of sugar significantly recorded higher alcohol percentage (15.72 %) over rest of the treatments followed by T3 with 40 % sugar (15.36 %). The treatment, T1 with 50 % of sugar recorded significantly lower alcohol percentage (14.53 %). The highest ascorbic acid content was recorded in T1 with 50% sugar (1.78 mg/100 g) followed by T2 with 45 % of sugar (1.63 mg/100 g) and lowest ascorbic acid content was recorded in T4 with 35% of sugar (1.58 mg/100 g). After six months of storage, quality of the wine regarding colour, taste, flavor and overall acceptability were increased to that of freshly processed wine. The benefit cost ratio of was calculated for the production of 1 kg of wine. Based on the results, formulation T3 secured the overall acceptability for sensory and nutritional evaluation (Uma Maheswari and Vidhu Valsan, 2019).

4. Apple wine

The results of ciders and wine prepared from culled apple fruits revealed that the cider prepared from combined variety was the best followed by 'Golden Delicious' and 'Red Delicious' varieties. In case of wine, 'Golden Delicious' variety was proved to be the best followed by combined variety and 'Red Delicious' varieties (Vyas and Kochhar, 1993). Sandhu *et al.* (1995) reported that the fermented beverages which could be prepared from apple are cider, wine and vermouth. Wine from apple was produced by subjecting the juice to alcoholic fermentation with an yield of about 11 per cent of alcohol.

5. Banana Wine

Producing wines by utilizing the surplus and excess bananas along with pectolase, sodium meta-bisulphite and passion fruit revealed that among the wines produced from different combinations, banana with pectolase, passion fruit with

sodium metabisulphite were found to be best with highest colour, best clarity and alcohol content of 13.65 per cent (Ronnie *et al.*, 2001). According to Jackson and Badrie (2003) 10 per cent of peel could be added to banana pulp for producing wine without significant quality changes of wines. The cell line studies were carried out with the processed red banana wine to determine the anti-cancer properties. The anti-cancer activity determination was carried over the HCT-15 colon cancer cell line. The red banana wine had capability of inhibiting the cell viability of the cancerous cells. The red banana wine showed its anti-cancer properties at the 0.63 % concentration whereas the cell viability was low when compared to other concentration and control (Uma Maheswari, 2020).

6. Carambola wine

Lakshmana *et al.* (2006) reported that carambola fruit pulp was diluted in the ratio of 1:2 was found to be best for fermentation. The pulp was ameliorated with cane sugar at different levels of 18°B, 20°B, 22°B, 24°B and 26°B. The sensory evaluation of wine showed that the wine prepared from must of 24°B was found to be the best.

7. Citrus wine

According to Singh *et al.* (1998) the production of alcohol from the kinnow juice was found to be good with *Saccharomyces cerevisiae* MTCC-178, when the soluble solids of the juices were set to 24° Brix, inoculum level at 14 % (v/v) and pH of 4.5 with fermentation temperature of 30 °C. Alobo (2002) studied some physicochemical changes associated with the fermentation of lemon juice. Analysis of the lemon juice showed that it had 0.70 % protein, 7.40°B Total Soluble Solids (TSS), 0.634 % Titratable Acidity (TA), 0.20 % ash, 62.0 mg/100 ml ascorbic acid and pH 3.97. The juice was added with diammonium monohydrogen-ortho-phosphate, potassium metabisulphite, ameliorated with sucrose sugar @ 22.5° B was inoculated with 3 % (v/v) yeast and fermented for 24 days. TSS and pH decreased while TA and alcohol increased with increasing period of fermentation.

8. Custard apple wine

Addition of 0.2 per cent pectinase was recommended for the better juice recovery from custard apple pulp and juice so obtained can be utilized for wine making and was comparable to that of grape wine (Kotecha *et al.* 1995).

9. Guava wine

Guava is a good source of ascorbic acid, pectin, sugars and certain minerals with widely appreciated flavour and aroma. Guava juice (221Brix) was fermented

with two different *S. cerevisiae* NCIM 3095 and NCIM3287strains and optimization of guava wine fermentation with respect to osmotolerance, alcohol tolerance, inoculums size, initial pH of the medium, amount of SO_2, amount of diammonium phosphate and incubation temperature were studied. For guava wine production, *S. cerevisiae* NCIM 3095 gave much better results (Sevda and Rodrigues, 2011).

10. Jamun wine

Sonar *et al.* (2004) reported that the optimum level of inoculum and pH of the must for the preparation of good quality jamun wine were at 5 and 3.5 per cent respectively. Lakshmana *et al.* (2008) reported the chemical composition of the wild jamun (*Syzygium fruitcosm*). The wine prepared from must inoculated with 6 % yeast culture and pH of 3.5 yielded higher ethanol content and maintained acceptable chemical composition and sensory quality.

11. Karonda wine

Karonda fruits of different ripening stages were used for the preparation of wine. The over-ripe Karonda fruits produced a beautiful, tasty and cherry red coloured wine with 8.26 per cent alcohol. The recovery of wine was about 438 ml/kg fruit (Bhajipale *et al.* 1998).

12. Mango wine

Mango wine was prepared by inoculating homogenized ripe mango pulp with *Saccharomyces cerevisiae* at 10 per cent inoculum level. The wine recorded 8.8 per cent of alcohol (Garg *et al.*, 1995). Mango varieties were evaluated for wine making. The pulp was allowed for fermentation inoculated with *Saccharomyces cerevisiae* var *ellipsoideous* No.522 for 10 to 12 days at ambient temperature. The wines made from 'Totapuri', 'Nekkare' and 'Mallika' mango varieties were excellent in quality. Sweet wines made from these varieties were also adjudged as good possessing characteristic fruity flavour (Thippesha *et al.*, 1997).

13. Palm wine

Palm wine produced with yeast *Saccharomyces cerevisiae* had characteristic odour while wine made with bacteria gave unfermented odour (Sylvia *et al.*, 1999).

14. Pomegranate wine

A good quality wine can be successfully prepared from pomegranate juice. The rate of fermentation of pomegranate juice was, however, slower than that of grape juice. The pomegranate wine had better flavour and colour than that of grape

wine (Adsule *et al.*, 1992). The juice extracted by hand press method with 5 per cent inoculum and pH 3.5 were found to be the optimum conditions for preparation of good quality pomegranate wine (Kumbhar *et al.,* 2002). Use of wine yeast, *Saccharomyces ellipsoideous* No.101 was suitable for preparation of home wine from pomegranate juice. The cultivars of pomegranate 'Ganesh', 'Arakta' and 'Kesar' were screened for wine production with FWY-4, FWY-6 and standard *Saccharomyces ellipsoideous* No.101. Arakta variety with standard wine yeast produced wine of superior quality over other two varieties. Pomegranate vermouth prepared from cardamom scored high rank followed by ginger and clove (Patil *et al.*, 2005). Ten strains of yeast were screened for pomegranate wine production. Strains FWY-4 and FWY-6 performed better with 8.25 and 7.80 per cent of alcohol respectively (Patil *et al.* 2006).

15. Pineapple wine

Two Pineapple varieties and three yeast strains were screened for wine production. The Queen variety with *S. ellipsoideous* No.101 recorded the highest score than Kew variety with same strain and that inoculated with SPQ-3 and SPQ-4 (Patil and Patil, 2006).

16. Plum wine

Sparkling wine produced from plum fruits and allowed to mature in bottles was more superior to that of stored in tanks (Joshi *et al.,* 1995).

17. Strawberry wine

Two varieties of strawberry namely, 'Sujatha' and 'Labella' were used for wine making with 10 % of inoculum. 'Sujatha' variety produced wine of acceptable quality and could be comparable with grape wine (Shravana Kumar *et al.*, 2001). The flavor profiling of wines made from three cultivars viz. 'Camarosa', 'Chandler' and 'Doughlas' were compared. The wine made from cultivars, 'Camarosa' and 'Chandler' had significantly higher flavour intensities over 'Doughlas' (Joshi *et al.*, 2006).

18. Sapota wine

According to Gautam and Chundawat (1998), reported that the wine prepared from different sapota juices (sapota pulp, non-clarified sapota juice and clarified sapota juice), the wine prepared either from the clarified or non-clarified sapota juice was highly acceptable. The sensory evaluation studies showed that the clarified juice wine had the highest score. Honde and Adsule (1998) observed that with increase in the level of yeast inoculum from 2 - 5 %, there was a significant

decrease in the TSS, total sugars and reducing sugar in the sapota wine. The alcohol content of the sapota wine was found to increase significantly with increase in inoculum levels from 2 – 5 %. The maximum alcohol content was observed at 5 % inoculum levels. The scores for sensory properties of wine were found to increase with increase in the level of inoculum from 2 – 5 %.

19. Conclusion

From the review, it is concluded that the utilization of fruits in the production of fruit wines is a viable alternative that allows the use of harvest surpluses, results in the introduction of value-added products into the market.

20. Reference

1) Adsule, R.N., P.M. Kotecha, and S.S. Kadam. 1992. Preparation of wine from pomegranate. Beverage & Food world, 19 (4): 13-14.
2) Alobo, A.P. 2002. Some physicochemical changes associated with the fermentation of lemon juice for wine production. Journal of Sustainable Agriculture and the Environment, 4(2): 216-223.
3) Bhajipale, B.J., D.N. Gupta, and V.B. Mehta. 1998. Effect of different stages of ripening of fruit on karonda wine. Indian Food Packer, 52(1):27-30.
4) Bisson, L.F., C.E. Butzke, and S.E. Ebeler. 1995. The role of moderate ethanol consumption in health and human nutrition. American J. Enol. Vitic., 48(4): 449-460.
5) Garg, N., D.K. Tandon, and S.K. Karla. 1995. Production of mango vinegar by immobilized cells of *Acetobacter aceti*. Journal of Food Science and Technology, 32(3): 216-218.
6) Gautam, S. K. and B.S. Chundawant. 1998. Standardization of technology of sapota wine making. Indian Food Packer, pp.17-21.
7) Ghadge, S.A., P.M. Kotecha, and J.K. Chavan. 2006. Studies on preparation of wine from grapes. Beverage and Food World, p.70.
8) Honde, V.M. and R.N. Adsule. 1998. Effect of inoculum levels on the chemical composition and sensory properties of sapota wine. Journal of Maharashtra Agricultural Universities., 23 (1): 89 – 90.
9) Jackson, T. and N. Badrie. 2003. Utilization of Banana (*Musa acuminata*) peel in wine produced in the Caribbean: Effects on physico-chemical, microbiological and sensory quality of wines. Journal of Food Science and Technology, 40(2): 153-156.

10) Jagtap, U.B., S.R. Waghmare, V.H. Lokhande, P. Suprasanna, and V.A. Bapat. 2011. Preparation and evaluation of antioxidant capacity of Jackfruit (*Artocarpus heterophyllus* Lam.) wine and its protective role against radiation induced DNA damage. Industrial Crops and Products, 34(3): 1595-1601.

11) Joshi, V.K., S.K. Sharma, and N.S. Thakur. 1995. Technology and quality of sparkling wine with special reference to plum an overview. Indian Food Packer., 49(3): 49-65.

12) Joshi, V.K., Somesh Sharma, and K. Kumar. 2006. Technology for production and evaluation of Strawberry wine. Beverage and Food World, pp.77-88.

13) Kotecha, P.M., R.N. Adsule, and S.S. Kadam. 1995. Processing of custard apple: Preparation of ready-to-serve beverages and wine. Indian Food Packer, pp.5-11.

14) Kumbhar, S.C., P.M. Kotecha, and S.S. Kadam. 2002. Effect of methods of juice extraction on the quality of pomegranate wine. Indian Food Packer, 51-52.

15) Kumoro, A.C., D. Rianasari, A.P.P. Pinandita, D.S. Retnowati, and C.S. Budiyati. 2012. Preparation of wine from Jackfruit (*Artocarpus heterophyllus* Lam.) juice using baker yeast: effect of yeast and initial sugar concentrations. World Applied Sciences Journal, 16(9): 1262-1268.

16) Lakshmana, D., B.A. Rahiman, and H.B. Lingaiah. 2006. Effect of quality of must on the quality of carambola wine. Karnataka Journal of Agriculture Science, 19(2): 352-356.

17) Lakshmana, D., B.A. Rahiman, and H.B. Lingaiah. 2008. Effect of different levels of pH and culture on quality of wild Jamun (*Syzygium fruitcosm*) fruit wine. Environment and Ecology, 26(4): 1759-1764.

18) Moreno-Arribas, M.V. and Polo, M.C.(2005).Winemaking biochemistry and microbiology: Current knowledge and future trends. Critical Reviews in Food Science and Nutrition, 45, 265–286.

19) Padshetty, M.S., R.B. Patil, M.S. Subba Rao, and B.L. Amla. 1982. Maturity stage and Harvest season effect on dry wine, variety, Bangalore Blue. Indian Food Packer, 36(1): 81-84.

20) Patil, A.B, S.S. Matapathi, Jones, P. Nirmalnath, and G. Sreenivasalu. 2006. Isolation and screening of efficient wine yeasts for pomegranate wine production. Beverage and Food World, pp.67-69.

21) Patil, A.B. and S.K. Patil. 2006. Technology development for wine making from pineapple. Beverage and Food world, pp.58 – 60.

22) Patil, A.B., S.S. Matapathi, Jones, P. Nirmalnath, M.K. Sheik, and S. Patil. 2005. Screening of pomegranate cultivars for wine production. Beverage and Food World, pp.56-58

23) Patil, A.B., S.S. Matapathi, Jones, P. Nirmalnath, M.K. Sheik, and S. Patil. 2005. Screening of pomegranate cultivars for wine production. Beverage and Food World, pp.56-58.

24) Ronnie, E. Brathwaite, and Neela, Badrie. 2001. Quality Changes in banana (*Musa acuminata*) wines on adding pectolase and passion fruit. Journal of Food Science and Technology, 38(4): 381-384.

25) Sandhu, D.K. and V.K. Joshi. 1995. Technology quality and scope of fruit wines especially apple beverages. Indian Food Industry, 24-34.

26) Sevda, S.B., and Rodrigues,L. 2011.Fermentative behavior of Saccharomyces strains during guava(*Psidium Guajava* L.) must fermentation and optimization of guava wine production. Journal of Food Processing&Technology, 2.

27) Shravana Kumar., R.G Maninegalai, and Hamaran. 2001. Wine preparation from strawberry. Beverage and Food World, pp.18-19.

28) Singh, M., P.S. Panesar, and S.S. Marwha. 1998. Studies on the suitability of Kinnow fruits for the production of wine. Journal of Food Science and Technology, 35(5): 455-457.

29) Sonar, R.P., S.D. Masalkar, V.K.Garnade, and R.S. Gaikwad. 2004. Influence of Inoculum levels and pH of the must on the quality of Jamun wine. Beverage Food World, pp. 69-70.

30) Suresh, E.R, S.Ethiraj, and S.S Negi. 1985. Evaluation of new grape cultivar for preparation of wine. Journal of Food Science and Technology, 22 (3): 211-212.

31) Sylvia, Uzochukwu, Esther, Balogh, O.G. Thucknot, M.J. Lewis, and P.O. Ngoddy. 1999. Role of palm wine yeasts and bacteria in palm wine aroma. Journal of Food Science and Technology, 36(4): 301-304.

32) Thippesha, D, V. Chikkasubbanna, and K.V. Jayaprasad. 1997. Evaluation of mango cultivars. Journal of the Science of Food and Agriculture, 43(5):230-235.

33) Uma Maheswari, T. and Vidhu Valsan. 2019. Quality analysis of jackfruit wine. International Journal of Life Sciences Research, 7 (1): 98-100.

34) Uma Maheswari, T., M.Karuppaiya, S. Subhagar, R. Rahul and P. Sivasakthivelan. 2020. Anti-cancer activity of red banana wine against colon cancer cells (HCT-15). Research Journal of Agricultural Sciences, 11(2): 420-423. March- April, 2020.

35) Vyas, K.K. and A.P.S. Kochhar.1993. Studies on cider and wine from culled apple fruit available in Himachal Pradesh. Indian Food Packer, 47(4): 15-21.

Scientific Advancements in Current Agricultural Research
ISBN: 978-81-947154-7-4
First Edition; 2020
Chapter – 6, Page: 64 - 71

6

INTENSIVE CULTIVATION TECHNOLOGY IN TROPICAL FRUIT CROPS

M. Rajkumar and T. Uma Maheswari[*]

Department of Horticulture, Faculty of Agriculture, Annamalai University, Annamalai Nagar, Tamil Nadu, India
E.mail: umahorti2003@gmail.com

Abstract

HDP is defined as planting at a density in excess of that which gives maximum crop yield at maturity if the individual tree grows to its full natural size. It is the planting of more number of plants than optimum through manipulation of tree size. Optimizing plant density per area and fertilization application are basic ways to practice scientific agriculture. These are essential for cost-effective and profitable crop production. HDP and meadow orcharding gives higher yield as well as returns /unit area due to increasing the number of trees/unit area. It is possible by regular pruning and use of bioregulators for maintaining the size and shape of the tree. HDP system is the fastest way of reducing the gestation period and simultaneously increasing the productivity of the orchards.

Key words: High Density Planting (HDP), Tropical fruit crops, Meadow orcharding and Intensive cultivation

1. Introduction

Optimizing plant density per area and fertilization application are basic ways to practice scientific agriculture. These are essential for cost-effective and profitable crop production. High density planting system (HDP) is exploited to increase yield

and thereby net return by accommodating higher number of plants in a given area. High density planting in fruit crops has been pioneered for temperate fruits in Europe at the end of 1960. It is of main concern to the growers with small landholding. High density planting is referred as semi-intensive system accommodating 500 - 1000 trees/ha. Intensive system accommodating 1000 - 10000 trees/ha employing specialized training systems and super intensive system is with 20000 - 100000 trees/ha. HDP is a very intensive form of fruit production which has high relevance to the food and nutritional security of our ever increasing population. HDP is defined as planting at a density in excess of that which gives maximum crop yield at maturity if the individual tree grows to its full natural size. It is the planting of more number of plants than optimum through manipulation of tree size (Saroj and Krishnan Kumar Singh, 2018).

2. Concept of High Density Planting

The exact limit of plant density to be termed as high density is not yet well defined. It varies with the region, species, variety, rootstock, cost of planting material, labour, likely return from the orchard, and agro techniques adopted for a particular crop. The underlying principle of High density planting is to make the best use of vertical and horizontal space per unit time and to harness maximum possible return per unit of inputs.

3. Principle of High Density Planting (HDP)

- To harness maximum possible returns per unit inputs and resources.
- Increased capture of sunlight per unit area.
- Land use efficiency.
- Appropriate vegetative and reproductive balance of the plants.
- To make the best use of vertical and horizontal space per unit time.

4. Important components of HDP

- Planting system
- Canopy Management
- Use of dwarfing rootstocks
- Training and Pruning
- Shoot Pruning
- Root Pruning
- Use of Growth Regulators

5. Planting system

It is aimed to achieve high assimilated production for its conversion into economic yield. Various planting systems adopted in fruit crops *viz.*, square,

triangular, quincunx, rectangular, hexagonal, hedgerow (single &double), paired planting and cluster planting. Square and triangular systems are followed for HDP in mango, kinnow, banana, papaya.

6. Training and Pruning

Pruning gives the dwarfing effect on the tree. Slow growing trees respond more favorably to pruning and training and can be maintained at a given size and shape without sacrificing yield. Removal of apical portion- gives compact and bushy tree. Mango, guava, citrus and most of the other fruit crops in India are evergreen and are seldom pruned. The training begins when the tree is first planted and continuous throughout its productive life. Proper tree forms, branch angle and limb spacing in it aids in growth control. First training is done after one growing season.

7. Advantages of HDP

- It induces precocity in bearing.
- Increases yield.
- Improves fruit quality.
- It reduces labour cost resulting in low cost of production.
- It also enables the mechanization of fruit crop production.
- It facilitates more efficient use of fertilizers, water, solar radiation, fungicide, weedicide, and pesticides.
- HDP technology results in maximization of unit area yield and availability of the fruits in the market early which fetch better price.

8. Light interception

In initial life of high density groove, this resource is effectively utilized as compared to conventional planting. However, in later years, the interception is poor due to crowding of tree canopy. It often results in smaller sized fruits and poor colour development.

9. Fruit size and quality

The yield is very high in dense planting. Fruit size may be relatively smaller with little or no effect on fruit quality.

10. Weed growth and population

Weeds are unwanted plants, which compete with for water, nutrients, Light and harbor insect pest and disease and interfere with orchard management and harvesting operation, resulting in poor growth and productivity of main crop. Due to

dense canopy in HDP only the filtered light is intercepted by the ground, which affected the weed growth and population per unit area. In the initial years of establishment, there may be some growth of weeds but in late years, the problem of weeds is eliminated.

11. Fruit maturity

One of the major effects of the HDP has been on the hastening or delaying of the fruit maturity. This effect can be effectively utilized by the farmers for harnessing maximizing profits from high density planting.

12. Incidence of Insect pest and disease

HDP changes the microclimate of the particular piece of land due to reduction in sunlight, affecting the temperature and humidity. These conditions are favorable for the occurrence or increase in the incidence or intensity of insect pests and disease.

13. Harvesting problems

Harvesting in high density planting is really a difficult task. In the initial years of the planting it may not be a problem, however, after full maturity of trees, harvesting may be a great problem. However, new approach like mechanical harvesting has become as one of the most viable option in high density planting than on convectional planting.

14. Spacing at different planting system in fruit crops

Crop	Normal spacing (m)	HDP spacing (m)	Meadow spacing (m)
Mango	7.5 x 7.5 - 12.5 x 12.5	3 x 2.5 – 5 x 5	2.5 x 2.5 – 3 x 1
Banana	2 x 2 – 2 x 3	1.5 x 1.5 - 1.8 x 1.8	1.2 x 1.2 – 3 x 0.5
Citrus	6 x 6 – 8 x 8	3 – 6 x 3 - 4.5	-
Papaya	2 x 2 – 3 x 3	1.8 x 1.8	1.2 x 1.2 – 1 x 1
Guava	6 x 6 – 8 x 8	3 x 3 – 3 x 1.5	2 x 2 – 2 x 1

Source: Saroj and Krishnan Kumar Singh, 2018

15. Dwarf scion varieties and Dwarf Rootstock varieties

Crop	Dwarf Scion Varieties	Dwarf Scion Features	Dwarf Rootstock Varieties
Mango	Amarapalli	Tends to bear regularly	Vellaikolumban, Alphonso, Olour, Himsagar, Langra
Citrus	-		*Citrangequat, Feronia* and *Severinia buxifolia,* Trifoliate orange, Sour orange, Citranges
Guava	-		*Psidium friedrichsthalianum, P. pumilum,* Aneuploid-82
Papaya	Pusa Nanha Dwarf	Tend to bear at lower height	

Source: Saroj and Krishnan Kumar Singh, 2018

Chapter - 6

16. HDP in Mango

The productivity of mango in India is comparatively less than other mango producing countries. The reasons for low productivity are as follows. Most of the commercial cultivars are location specific with long generation period with alternate bearing habit *viz.* Deshehari, Langra, chausa, Bombaygreen, Alphonso, Banganapalli, Pairi, Himsagar, kesar, Mulgoa etc. The normal planting distance for conventional mango planting is ranging from 10-12m due to poor soil conditions. Most of Mango orchards are rain fed and seldom applied with nutrients. Controlling tree size by dwarfing rootstocks in High Density orchards is one of the methods of increasing production. In HDP yields are improved in early life of orchard life. High Density Planting (3 m x 3 m) produced almost ten times more yield as compared to normal system of planting (10 m x 10 m). So, High Density Planting is found promising for commercial cultivation to traditional system of planting.

According to Dalvi *et al.* (2010), the experiment was conducted to study the flowering and yield parameters in Alphonso mango as influenced by HDP. The result showed that highest yield was recorded in the spacing of 5 m x 5 m. According to Sunil and Chalak (2017), the experiment was conducted to study the effect of high density planting systems on fruit weight and fruit quality of Amrapali mango. The Maximum yield (11.80 kg) was recorded in Double hedge row system. The highest monetary returns (Rs.3,72,312/-ha) and the highest B:C ratio (3.3) was recorded in the spacing 5 x 5 m and it was followed by the spacing 5 x 10 m (2.5).

According to Sanjay *et al.* (2001), the experiment was conducted to study the effect of plant spacing on growth, yield and quality of mango cv Kesar. The result showed that all the parameters recorded highest in the spacing of 10 x 10 m (100).

17. HDP in Banana

Banana is the fourth important food ingredient in terms of gross value next to rice, wheat and milk product. The normal spacing provided in Robusta and Dwarf Cavendish is 2.1 x 2.1 m (2267 plant/ha) with yield of 60 tonnes/ha. This can be done under good management condition where micro irrigation and Drip fertigation could be conveniently and successfully practiced. HDP in Banana is a practice to accommodate 4444 to 5555 plants per ha and yield is recorded to be in order of 80 - 120 tons per ha depends on variety. But, main limiting factor in Banana under HDP is the sunlight, which influences flowering, crop duration, maturity and performance of ratoon crop. According to Gogai *et al.* (2015), the experiment was conducted to study the effect of HDP in pseudostem height (cm) and girth (cm), total number of

leaves, functional leaves, leaf area and leaf area Index of Banana . The result showed that 2 or 3 suckers per hill registered higher number of functional leaves.

18. HDP in Citrus

HDP technology is gaining popularity in citrus because of earlier production and net returns, increasing land values and higher taxes of land, efficient use of nutrient and water due to greater root densities, efficient pesticidal application and easier weed control. The seedlings of acid lime cv. Pramalini plantation was evaluated under Ultra-High Density Planting (UHD - 1600 trees ha^{-1} at 2.5 × 2.5 m) and high density planting (HDP - 800 trees ha^{-1} at 5 × 2.5 m) systems over conventional or control (CON - 400 trees ha^{-1} at 5 × 5 m) planting spacing. Dense and vigorous plant canopy with maximum (1.49) leaf area index was found in HDP and lowest was under UHD (1.18). Although insect – pest and disease incidence were higher in close spacing plantation than CON, physico-chemical fruit parameters were not affected by spacing. The fruit yield on per plant basis was always significantly lowest under UHD. However, on area basis, under UHD plantation fruit yield (8.24 - 35.36 t ha^{-1}) was more than two folds as compared to control (3.08 - 11.64 t ha^{-1}) for different years. Although during last year of experiment the yield under Ultra-High Density Planting (35.36 t ha^{-1}) was significantly higher than high density planting (25.09 t ha^{-1}), the B:C ratio was nearly similar in both the cases. Therefore, it may concluded that the high density planting system may be preferred during early years of production as reported by Ladaniya *et al.* (2019).

19. HDP in Guava

Guava is successfully grown all over India. The total area and production of guava in the country are 1.90 lakh hectare and 1.68 million tonnes. The most popular guava cultivars are Lucknow 49, Allahabad safeda and Harijha. According to Kumawat *et al.* (2014), the experiment was conducted to study the effect of different spacing on newly planted cv. L-49 under UHDP system. The result shows that the spacing of 2.0 x 1.5 m recorded the highest fruit set and fruit weight was more in 2.0 x 2.0 m spacing. Intensive density of planting system, that is, 2 × 1 m spacing recorded satisfactory growth, light interception below significantly higher number of flower plant^{-1}, fruit weight, TSS/acid ratio and estimated yield ha^{-1} with optimum plant per unit area (5000 ha^{-1}).

20. Meadow Orcharding (UHDP)

Very high productivity with superior fruit quality is achieved with Meadow orcharding. Plants spaced at 1 x 2 m accommodate 5000 plants per hectare; canopy management through topping and hedging. Plants are topped 2 months of planting in

October for emergence of new shoots below cut end. 50 % length of each new shoots, pruned again in December - January for induction of more shoots; flower buds differentiate; well spread is attained by May. Heading back of all shoots is repeated annually in September, May and January; ensures dwarf, compact canopy, better fruiting and easy horticultural operations. Production starts from very first year of planting, 12.5 tonnes reaching up to 55 tonnes per hectare. Lalit performs very well under UHDP (Gorakh Singh, 2008).

21. HDP in Papaya

Papaya originated from tropical America, has become a popular fruit due to its fast growth, high yield, long fruiting period high nutrient value as well. In addition, it has been used as vegetable, Fruit processing, and papain production at immature stage. It can be a highly profitable crop now. Pusa Nanha is a dwarfing variety. Spacing followed for Pusa Nanha is 1.2 x 1.2. This study was conducted at Central Mindanao University to determine the effects of varying planting densities and nutrient rates on the growth and fruit set of 'Solo' papaya. Planting densities (plants per ha or pph) served as Factor A. Nutrient rates in reference to a recommended rate (RR) as Factor B. The experiment was arranged in a 3 x 3 factorial in RCBD with three replications. Plants in 3,333 pph with 50 % nutrient RR were the tallest amongst treatment combinations at 8 MAT and 10 MAT. Those in 2,500 pph with 100% nutrient RR had widest stems at flowering stage. Plants in 3,333 pph formed longest flowers and fruits with 150% nutrient RR. Highest fruit count per plant was recorded in 2,000 pph at 8 MAT. As per hectare basis, highest planting density produced the most number of developed fruits (117,217) at 6 MAT. However, fruit count per hectare was comparable for all planting densities and nutrient rates at 8 MAT (Valleser, 2016).

22. HDP in Sapota

According to Thirupathaiah *et al.* (2017), the experiment was conducted to study the effect of micronutrients on fruit yield of sapota. It can be concluded that application of RDF + 0.5 % $ZnSO_4$ + 0.5 % $FeSO_4$ + 0.3 % B per tree through foliar application can be recommended for increased growth (height, spread, and tree volume), yield and economy of sapota cv. Kalipatti under high density planting systems for fruits without any adverse effect on the environment, and also it will promote increased productivity by the timely availability of required nutrients.

23. Conclusion

HDP and meadow orcharding gives higher yield as well as returns /unit area due to increasing the number of trees/unit area. It is possible by regular pruning and use of bioregulators for maintaining the size and shape of the tree. HDP system is the fastest way of reducing the gestation period and simultaneously increasing the productivity of the orchards.

24. Reference

1) Dalvi, N.V., B. R. Salvi, S. A. Chavan and M. P. Kandalkar. 2010. High density planting in Mango cv. Alphonso. J.Hort.Sci.,5(2):117-119.

2) Gogoi,B., B. Khangia, K. Baruah and A. Khound. 2015. Effect of HDP and Nutrient Management on Growth and Yield of banana cv. Jahoji. International Journal of Agriculture Innovations and Research, 3(5): 2319 - 1473.

3) Gorakh Singh. 2008. High Density and Meadow orcharding of guava. Extension Bulletin-35, Central Institute for Subtropical Horticulture, Lucknow, Director Central Institute for Subtropical Horticulture, Rehmankhera, P.O. Kakori, Lucknow - 227 107, pp.1-20.

4) Kumawat, K. L., D. K. Sarolia, R. A. Kaushik and A. S. Jodha. 2014. Effect of different spacing on newly planted guava cv. L- 49 under ultra high density planting system. African Journal of Agricultural Research, 9(51): 3729 - 3735.

5) Ladaniya M. S., R. A. Marathe, A. K. Das, C. N. Rao, A. D. Huchche, P. S. Shirgure and A. A. Murkute. 2019. High density planting studies in acid lime (*Citrus aurantifolia* Swingle). Scientia Horticulturae, 261.

6) Sanjay, S., G. S. Yadav and M. N. Hoda. 2001. High density planting system in Amrapali mango. Indian Journal of Agricultural Sciences,71(6): 381 - 390.

7) Saroj, S. A and K. Krishnan Kumar Singh. 2018. Density concept of orcharding. International Journal of Advanced Scientific Research and Management, 22(1): 250 - 263.

8) Sunil, C and S. Chalak. 2017. Effect of spacing on Growth, Yield and Quality of Mango. J. Krishi Vigyan, 5(2): 340 - 352.

9) Thirupathaiah, G., P. Sampath, M. Shirol, A.M. Bhaskar Rao, B. Nirmala. and A.K. Sumangala Koulagi. 2017. Influence of micronutrients on growth, yield and economy of sapota cv. kalipatti under HDP system. International Journal of Agricultural Science and Research,7(3): 401 - 408.

10) Vences C. Valleser. 2016. Planting densities and nutrient rates on the growth and fruit set of 'Solo' Papaya (*Carica papaya* L.). CMUJS, 20(3): 54 - 68.

Scientific Advancements in Current Agricultural Research
ISBN: 978-81-947154-7-4
First Edition; 2020
Chapter – 7, Page: 72 - 81

7

MULTIPLE GENE TRANSFER IN VEGETABLE CROPS

M. Venkatraman*, D. Anbarasi and K. Haripriya

Department of Horticulture, Faculty of Agriculture, Annamalai University, Annamalai Nagar, Tamilnadu, India.
*Corresponding author: venkatraman854@gmail.com

Abstract

Vegetable crop species are grown worldwide to provide a source of fiber, nutrients and vitamins in the human diet. Genetic transformation for the introduction of foreign genes to enhance resistance to insect pests and fungal diseases has been accomplished for at least 19 vegetable crop species belonging to 8 botanical families. Although, some reports of genetically engineered vegetable crop species are limited to expression of selectable marker genes, there are many reports, described here, that have demonstrated the expression of genes which encode potentially useful agronomic and horticultural traits. These include enhanced resistance to insect pests through the expression of *Bacillus thuringensis* crystalline endotoxins and trypsin inhibitors. Enhanced resistance to fungal pathogens has been achieved through the expression of antifungal proteins and various other antimicrobial compounds, while virus resistance has been achieved through coat-protein mediated expression. Transgenic vegetable crops with enhanced resistance to pests and diseases should become a part of an integrated pest management program in the future. Available plant transformation methods include indirect (i.e., requiring an intermediate biological vector, usually the bacterium *Agrobacterium tumefaciens*) and direct methods (electroporation or PEG-mediated transformation of protoplasts, biolistics, etc.).

Key words: Genetic engineer, *Bacillus thuringensis* and *Agrobacterium tumefaciens*

1. Introduction

Vegetable crop species are grown worldwide to provide a source of fiber, nutrients and vitamins in the human diet. Genetic transformation for the introduction of foreign genes to enhance resistance to insect pests and fungal diseases has been accomplished for at least 19 vegetable crop species belonging to 8 botanical families. Although some reports of genetically engineered vegetable crop species are limited to expression of selectable marker genes, there are many reports, described here, that have demonstrated the expression of genes which encode potentially useful agronomic and horticultural traits. These include enhanced resistance to insect pests through the expression of *Bacillus thuringensis* crystalline endotoxins and trypsin inhibitors. Enhanced resistance to fungal pathogens has been achieved through the expression of antifungal proteins and various other antimicrobial compounds, while virus resistance has been achieved through coat-protein mediated expression. Transgenic vegetable crops with enhanced resistance to pests and diseases should become a part of an integrated pest management program in the future.

Vegetable crop species are grown worldwide and provide an important source of fiber, nutrients and vitamins in the human diet. They are consumed fresh or may be eaten after cooking, processing of pickling, and constitute an important part of the meals of billions of people. The crops may be grown under field conditions or under controlled environment conditions, such as in greenhouses. A large number of vegetable crop species have been genetically transformed, and they belong to at least 8 different taxonomic families.

Most crops are annual or infrequently biennial plants (such as carrot); a few species are perennial (such as asparagus and watercress). The edible portions of these plants represent the complete spectrum of botanical features, including root (beet, carrot), stem (asparagus), tuber (potato), leaf (cabbage, chicory, lettuce, spinach, watercress), flower (broccoli, cauliflower) and fruit (cucumber, eggplant, pepper, tomato). Significant progress has already been made using conventional breeding strategies to produce horticulturally improved, high-yielding and nutritionally-enhanced cultivars of virtually all of the vegetable crops presently grown under cultivation.

In addition, resistance to insect pests and diseases, and enhanced tolerance to environmental stresses, have been incorporated using conventional breeding methods [see also – Conventional Plant Breeding for Higher Yields and Pest Resistance]. This has resulted in vegetable crop species being cultivated in a wide range of environments and niches throughout the world. With the advent of recent techniques in genetic engineering that now permit the introduction into plants of

foreign genes through transformation; these methods have been utilized to introduce additional genes to potentially enhance the horticultural quality of vegetable crops. In this chapter, the general approaches used to transform vegetable crop species and examples of crops with specific traits to enhance insect pest and fungal and viral disease resistance are described.

2. Gene Pyramiding Concept

First introduced the concept called gene pyramiding. Gene pyramiding is defined as a method aimed at assembling multiple desirable genes from multiple parents into a single genotype. The end product of a gene pyramiding program is a genotype with all of the target genes (Burgal *et al.,* 2008).

3. Objectives of Gene pyramiding include

- Enhancing trait performance by combining two or more complementary genes
- Remedying deficits by introgressing genes from other sources
- Increasing the durability.

4. Types of Gene Pyramiding

- *Serial gene pyramiding:* Genes are deployed in same plant one after other.
  - ✓ Pedigree breeding
  - ✓ Backcross breeding
  - ✓ Recurrent selection

- *Simultaneous gene pyramiding:* Genes are deployed at a time in a single plant.
  - ✓ Marker assisted selection
  - ✓ Transgenic method

5. Conventional technique

Conventional Breeding & Marker based gene pyramiding

- It is necessary to have the QTL of interest/target in the crossing breeding germplasm.
- The QTL should be able to give the expected level of product/product characteristics. e.g. Target yield, level of resistance/tolerance to biotic/abiotic stresses/level of production of valuable compounds like vitamins, AA, alkaloids, etc).

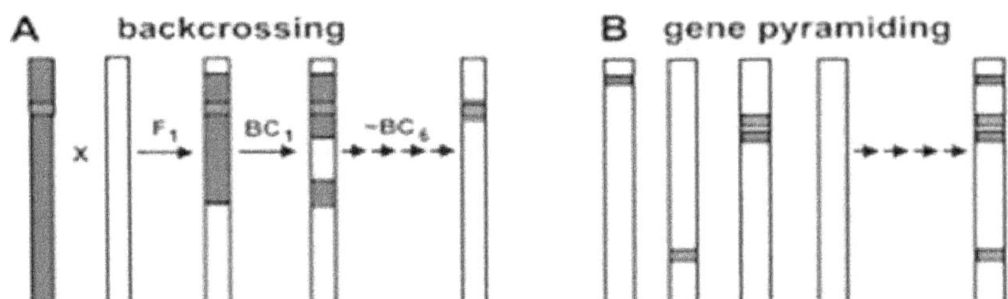

Disadvantage of Conventional breeding

a) Gene pyramiding is mainly used to improve qualitative traits such as disease and insect resistance. This is associated with the fact that the presence of target trait genes must be confirmed by phenotyping mostly at the individual level and that individual phenotypic performance is a good indicator of the genotype only if genes have a major effect on phenotypic performance and the error of phenotyping is minimal.

b) In addition to the reliability of phenotyping at individual level other factors influencing the success of gene pyramiding are the inheritance model of the genes for the target traits, linkage and/or pleiotropism between the target trait and other traits.

c) For instance, allelic genes cannot be combined in the same genotype. The effect conferred by a recessive gene cannot be evaluated on heterozygous individuals and progeny testing is required.

d) If the target gene is tightly linked to genes with large negative effects on other traits, these undesirable genes may be transferred together with the target gene into the recipient line and result in reduced performance of other traits (linkage drag). Therefore, any improvement in the knowledge of the trait genetics (inheritance, genetic relationship, etc.) and techniques for inferring genotype-phenotype relationship will be useful.

6. Marker Assisted Gene Pyramiding

Marker-assisted selection (MAS) is a method of rapidly incorporating valuable traits into new cultivars. Molecular markers, or DNA tags, that have been shown to be linked to traits of interest are particularly useful for incorporating genes that are highly affected by the environment, genes for resistance to diseases and pests, and to accumulate multiple genes for resistance to specific diseases and pests within the same cultivar – a process called gene pyramiding (Servin *at el.,* 2002).

Chapter - 7

7. Distinct Gene Pyramiding Scheme

In a gene pyramiding scheme, strategy is to cumulate into a single genotype, genes that have been identified in multiple parents. The use of DNA markers, which permits complete gene identification of the progeny at each generation, increases the speed of pyramiding process. In general, the gene pyramiding aims at the derivation of an ideal genotype that is homozygous for the favorable alleles at all the loci. The gene pyramiding scheme can be distinguished into two parts (Figure). The first part is called a pedigree, which aims at cumulating of all target genes in a single genotype called the root genotype. The second part is called the fixation step which aims at fixing the target genes into a homozygous state i.e. to derive the ideal genotype from the one single genotype. Each node of the tree is called an intermediate genotype and has two parents. Each of this intermediate genotype variety can resist. Moreover, pyramiding can also improve becomes a parent in the next cross. The intermediate genotypes are not just an arbitrary offspring of a given cross but it is a particular genotype selected from among the offspring in which all parental target genes are present.

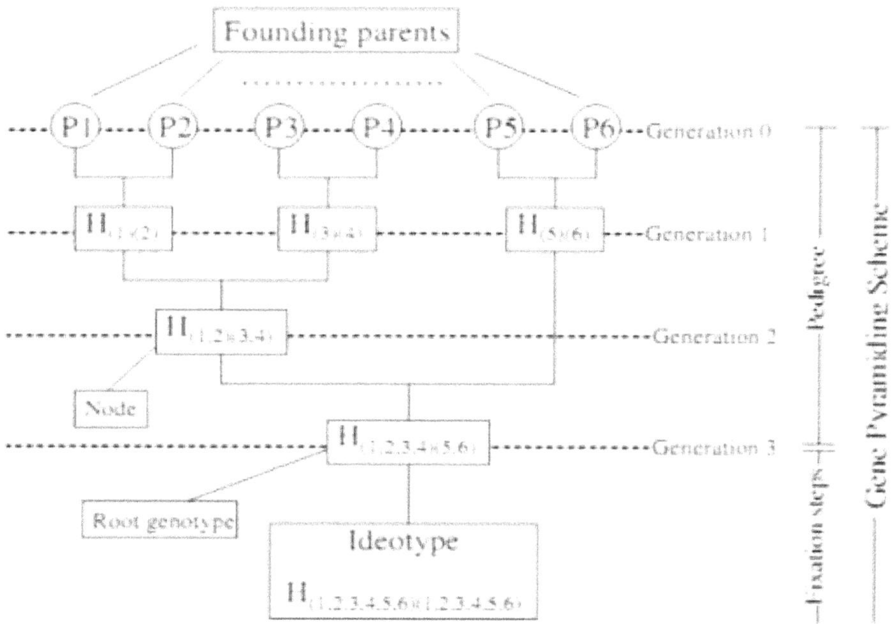

Although, the pedigree step may be common, several different procedures can be used to undergo fixation in gene pyramiding. Generation of a population of doubled haploids from the root genotype is a possible procedure for the fixation steps. Here, a population of gametes is obtained from the genotypes and their genetic material is doubled. This leads to a population of fully homozygous individuals,

among which the ideotype can be found. Using this process, the ideal genotype can be obtained in just one additional generation after the root genotype is obtained. However, producing large population of doubled haploid is difficult and cumbersome in certain plant species. A possible alternative to this method is to self the root genotype directly to obtain the ideal genotype. However, selfing the root genotype will result in the breakage of linkage between the desired alleles and it will be difficult to derive this breaks as the linkage phase is rarely visible in selfed populations. As a result, it may span too many generations thereby, stretching the gene pyramiding scheme. Another alternative to all this methods would be to obtain a genotype carrying all favorable alleles in coupling by crossing the root genotype with parent containing none of the favorable alleles. This confirms that the linkage phase of the offspring is known and the genotype can be derived without any mixing. The ideal genotype will be reached within two generations after the root genotype. However, instead of crossing with a blank parent, a more simplified method would be to cross the root genotype with one of the founding parents. In such programs, the linkage will still be known, and the selection will be for genotypes that are homozygous for the target gene brought by the founding parent but heterozygous for other regions. The desired genes need not be fixed subsequently, thereby increasing the probability of getting the ideal genotype. This is called as marker assisted backcross gene pyramiding. By far this is the most accepted and efficient method to do the gene pyramiding.

8. Marker Assisted Backcrossing

Breeders transfer a target allele from a donor variety to a popular cultivar by a repetitive process called backcrossing; which, unfortunately, is slow and uncertain. Breeding a plant that has the desired donor allele but otherwise looks just like the popular cultivar usually takes four years or longer. Worse, the augmented variety may look just like the popular cultivar, but it inevitably retains stray chromosome segments from the donor. Consequently, to a greater or lesser extent, it will fail to perform exactly like the popular cultivar, thus limiting its appeal to farmers. Marker- assisted breeding tackles both problems by allowing breeders to identify young plants with the desired trait and by facilitating the removal of stray donor genes from intermediate backcrosses. The result, in about two years, is an improved variety exactly like the popular cultivar except that it possesses the transferred advantageous gene. In principle, this technique can be applied to the breeding of any crop or farm animal. So far, however, breeders of trees and rice have dominated the field. Because markers allow breeders to select immature plants, the time saved in breeding slow-growing trees is immense.

In the case of rice, the crop's relatively advanced state of genetic mapping has facilitated the application of molecular marker techniques. Markers are effective aids to selection in backcrossing in three ways. First, markers can aid selection on target alleles whose effects are difficult to observe phenotypically. Examples include recessive genes, multiple disease resistance gene pyramids combined in one genotype (where they can epistatically mask each other's effects), alleles that are not expressed in the selection environments (e.g., genes conferring resistance to a disease that is not regularly present in environments), etc. Second, markers can be used to select for rare progeny in which recombination near the target gene have produced chromosomes that contain the target allele and as little possible surrounding DNA from the donor parent. Third, markers can be used to select rare progeny that are the result of recombination near the target gene, thus minimizing the effects of linkage drag. In general, the marker assisted backcross based gene pyramiding can be performed in three strategies (Figure 2). In the first method, the recurrent parent (RP1) is crossed with donor parent (DP1) to produce the F1 hybrid and backcrossed up to third backcross generation (BC3) to produce the improved recurrent parent (IRP1). This improved recurrent parent is then crossed with other donor parent (DP2) to pyramid multiple genes. This strategy is less acceptable as it is time taking but pyramiding is very precise as it involve one gene at one time. In the second strategy, the recurrent parent (RP1) is crossed with donor parents (DP1, DP2, etc.) to get the F1 hybrids which are then intercrossed to produce improved F1 (IF1) (Francia *et al.,*2005). This improved F1 is then backcrossed with the recurrent parent to get the improved recurrent parent (IRP). As such, the pyramiding is done in the pedigree step itself. However, when the donor parents are different, this method is less likely to be used because there is chance that the pyramided gene may be lost in the process. The third strategy is an amalgamation of the first two which involve simultaneous crossing of recurrent parent (RP1) with many donor parents and then backcrossing them up to the BC3 generation. The backcross populations with the individual gene are then intercrossed with each other to get the pyramided lines. This is the most acceptable way as in this method not only time is reduced but fixation of genes is fully assured. Marker assisted backcrossing to be effective, depends upon several factors, including the distance between the closest markers and the target gene, the number of target genes to be transferred, the genetic base of the trait, the number of individuals that can be analyzed and the genetic background in which the target gene has to be transferred, the type of molecular marker(s) used, and available technical facilities (Bertrand Servin *et al.,* 2004). When these entire selection criterions are

Chapter - 7

maintained properly, only then a well acceptable MAB based gene pyramiding scheme can lead to durable crop improvement.

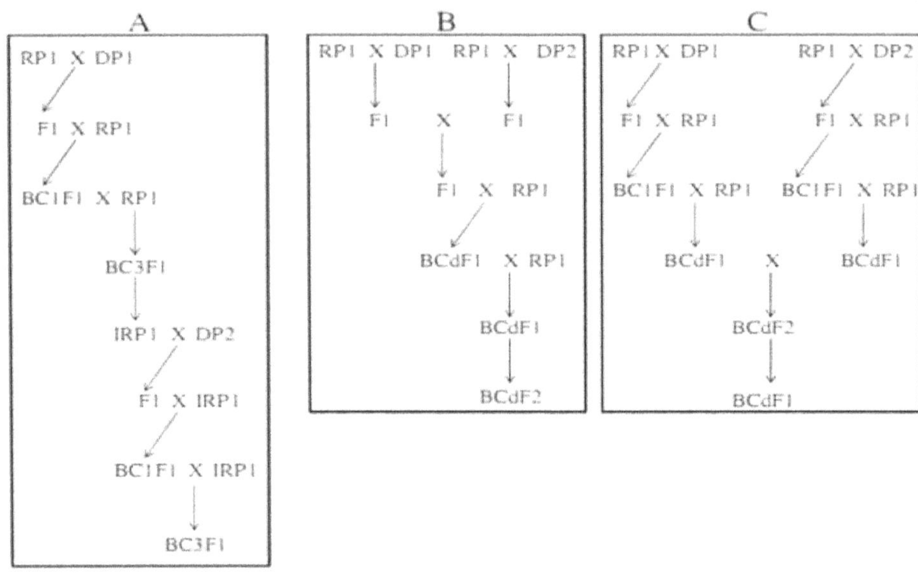

9. Gene transfer technologies

There are two approaches for achieving plant transformation, one involving an indirect means of gene transfer using Agrobacterium vectors and the second by direct methods using physical or electrical means of gene transfer.

Agrobacterium - mediated transformation

Agrobacterium tumefaciens, the causal agent of crown gall disease, infects plant cells to make them tumorigenic at the site of infection. Tumor cells contain genetic material unique to the bacterium. Research beginning in the 1970's revealed that A. tumefaciens is attracted to wounded plant tissues, attaches itself to the host and transfers a sequence of DNA harboring specific genes (T-DNA) from a large tumor-induding (Ti) plasmid. This process is mediated by a set of bacterial virulence genes on the Ti-plasmid whose expression is induced by host plant phenolic compounds eg: acetosyringone, which are produced at wound sites. The T-DNA enters the plant nucleus, integrates into the host genome and is subsequently expressed. Genes within the foreign DNA are then expressed to produce plant growth regulators (auxins and cytokinins), which cause uncontrollable cell growth and result in the production of tumors. Furthermore, the integration of the T-DNA fragment is also responsible for the synthesis of opines, which are amino acid and sugar derivatives that are metabolized by the Agrobacterium while living within the tumor. By the early 1980's, biotechnologists were exploiting the natural ability of the biological vector to transfer foreign genes into plant cells. Agrobacterium-mediated transformation is

simple and reliable and is the most commonly used method for vegetable crop transformation; however, it is limited by the bacterium's host range, since gene delivery has been predominantly successful with susceptible dicotyledonous species whereas monocots are generally not infected. Recently, Agrobacterium-mediated transformation of some monocots was demonstrated using highly embryogenic tissues and efficient selection protocols. While Allium species were previously regarded as recalcitrant to transformation and regeneration, reports of onion transformed by Agrobacterium are available and stable transgenic garlic has been devolped.   In contrast, A. rhizogenes is a soil bacterium that causes hairy root disease in wounded dicotylendonous plants and is a natural vector with the ability to transfer a specific segment of DNA in a similar manner to A. tumefaciens. Recently, there has been interest in using this vector for stable transformation of foreign genes into vegetable crop plants. A. rhizogenes carries a large root-inducing (Ri) plasmid harboring a T- DNA region. Integration and expression of Ri T-DNA into plant cells exploits similar mechanisms as A. tumefaciens-mediated gene delivery. Transformants can be selected by the development of hairy roots on hormone-free media or by the expression of an inserted foreign gene within the T-DNA region. However, transgenic plants regenerated from hairy roots may show altered phenotypes characterized by changes in life cycle, late flowering, higher growth rates, reduced fertility and morphological changes involving increased rooting, dwarfing and wrinkled leaves. A. rhizogenes- mediated transformation has been achieved with several vegetable crops and foreign genes to enhance resistance to insects have been expressed in cruciferous crops, including broccoli, cabbage and cauliflower (Ferry *et al.,* 2004).

Direct methods for Transformation

a) Particle bombardment (Biolistics)

This method was invented to overcome the obstacles of transforming plants that were not amenable to A. tumefaciens gene delivery. At present, the use of this transformation method is second to that of A. tumefaciens. Particle (microprojectile) bombardment involves accelerating DNA-coated microscopic gold or tungsten particles into target cells, where the genetic material integrates into the genome and results in the stable expression of the foreign gene. Microprojectile bombardment is the only transformation technique that can be applied to almost any cell or tissue type. The methodologies are simple and identical regardless of the target cells or DNA used. This method has been used to obtain genetically engineered bean and asparagus plants.

b) Protoplast-mediated transformation

DNA uptake into protoplasts relies on the temporary removal of the plant cell wall which functions as the principal barrier impeding foreign DNA entry into the cell. Removal of the plant cell wall is carried out enzymatically. The resulting protoplast becomes more amenable to DNA uptake by physical and chemical means that create pores in the cell membrane eg. electroporation, thereby allowing molecules to pass inside the cell. Once the foreign gene enters the plant cell, the membrane pores reseal, the cell wall is regenerated and the intact cell is induced to multiply to form callus, from which clones of transgenic plantlets can be regenerated.

An alternative to electroporation is a chemical means of DNA uptake involving polyethylene glycol (PEG). PEG in combination with divalent cations, such as calcium or magnesium, induce DNA uptake into protoplasts. The introduction of DNA into protoplasts by electroporation or PEG-mediated uptake potentially allows for the production of very large numbers of transformed cells; however, success is limited by difficulties in culturing protoplasts and achieving plant regeneration. This method has been used to produce transgenic plants of sweet potato.

10. Reference

1) Burgal J, Shockey J and Lu C. (2008). Metabolic engineering of hydroxy fatty acid production in plants: RcDGAT2 drives dramatic increases in ricinoleate levels in seed oil. Plant Biotechnology Journal, 6: 819 - 831.

2) Bertrand Servin, Olivier C. Martin, Marc Mezard and Frederic Hospital. (2004). Toward a Theory of Marker-Assisted Gene Pyramiding. Genetics Society of America.

3) Ferry, N., Edwards, M. G., Mulligan, E. A., Emami, K., Petrova, A. S., Frantescu, M., Davison, G. M and Gatehouse, A. M. R. (2004). Engineering resistance to insect pests. In: Christou P, Klee H (eds). Handbook of Plant Biotechnology. Vol. 1. John Wiley and Sons, Chichester, pp. 373 - 394.

4) Francia, E., Tacconi, G., Crosatti, C., Barabaschi, D., Bulgarelli, D., Dall' Aglio E and Vale, G. (2005). Marker assisted selection in crop plants. Plant. Cell. Tissue. Organ. Cult. 82: 317 - 342.

5) Hospital, F., I. Goldringer and S. Openshaw. 2000. Efficient marker-based recurrent selection for multiple quantitative traitloci. Genet. Res. 75: 357 – 368.

6) Servin, B and F. Hospital. 2002. Optimal positioning of markers to control genetic background in marker-assisted backcrossing. J. Hered., 93(3): 214 - 217.

Scientific Advancements in Current Agricultural Research
ISBN: 978-81-947154-7-4
First Edition; 2020
Chapter – 8, Page: 82 - 89

8

ROLE OF BIOTECHNOLOGICAL TOOLS IN HORTICULTURAL CROPS

K. Ramkumar[1] and S. Anuja[2]

Department of Horticulture, Faculty of Agriculture, Annamalai University, Annamalai Nagar, Tamil Nadu, India

*Corresponding author: ramkumarfarmercdm@gmail.com

Abstract

Biotechnological tools have revolutionized the entire crop improvement programmes by providing new strains of plants, supply of planting material, more efficient and selective pesticides and improved fertilizers. Many genetically modified horticultural crops such as fruits, vegetables, flowers, medicinal and aromatic crops are already in the market in developed countries. It is a new aspect of biological and agricultural science which provides new tools and strategies in the struggle against world's food production problem. The major areas of biotechnology which can be adopted for improvement of horticultural crops.

Key words: Tissue culture, Embryo culture, Meristem culture, Mutation and Pest resistance.

1. Introduction

Biotechnology will have a major impact on agriculture in coming decades. A whole spectrum of gene technology is now routinely and successfully applied to a wide range of problems in agriculture and horticulture. Research strategies need to be directed towards production of quality fruits in the horticulture area. We have to achieve success in several fruit varieties with delayed ripening and extended shelf life

and further our research efforts for increased synthesis of lycopene and beta carotene which act as strong antioxidants in tomato. Other climacteric fruit crops for extended shelf life are mango and banana. As many of the fruit crops provide a great deal of health benefit, much of the research efforts need to be focused on improvement of the nutritional quality. Therefore, there is a greater need to promote and accelerate the effort for mobilizing the tools of biotechnological and genetic engineering for improving the productivity stability and sustainability of our major fruit crops (Koundal, 2004).

Biotechnological tools have revolutionized the entire crop improvement programmes by providing new strains of plants, supply of planting material, more efficient and selective pesticides and improved fertilizers. Many genetically modified fruits and vegetables are already in the market in developed countries. Modern biotechnology encompasses broad areas of biology from utilization of living organisms or substances from those organisms to make or to modify a product, to improve plant or animal or to develop micro-organisms for specific use. It is a new aspect of biological and agricultural science which provides new tools and strategies in the struggle against world's food production problem. The major areas of biotechnology which can be adopted for improvement of horticultural crops are

2. Tissue Culture

One of the widest applications of biotechnology has been in the area of tissue culture and micro propagation in particular. It is one of the most widely used techniques for rapid asexual *in vitro* propagation. This technique is economical in time and space affords greater output and provides disease free and elite propagules. It also facilitates safer and quarantined movements of germplasm across nations. When the traditional methods are unable to meet the demand for propagation material this technique can produce millions of uniformly flowering and yielding plants.

Micropropagation of almost all the fruit crops and vegetables is possible now. Production of virus free planting material using meristem culture has been made possible in many horticultural crops. Embryo rescue is another area where plant breeders are able to rescue their crosses which would otherwise abort. Culture of excised embryos of suitable stages of development can circumvent problems encountered in post zygotic incompatibility.

3. Meristem culture

Garlic and shallot, which are propagated vegetatively, are known to harbor a number of viruses. Some of these viruses are latent, i.e., cause no visible symptoms, whereas others reduce yield considerably. However, meristem culture enables scientists to eliminate viruses in garlic and shallot. The dark-green "island" areas of the growing point (meristem) are either free of virus or to contain virus only low concentrations, by taking 0.3 mm meristems under aseptic conditions and culturing them on a suitable medium, virus-free garlic and shallot plants can be obtained. In conjunction with the vigorous virus testing scheme, 25 garlic and 6 shallot lines have been so far obtained to be free from onion yellow dwarf virus, garlic common latent virus, shallot latent virus, and leek yellow strip virus. This shall assure that all incoming and outgoing garlic and shallot germplasm is free of virus. The yield of one of two meristem-derived, virus-free line was 76 % higher than that of the field-propagated line. This technique also facilitates international exchange of disease-free germplasm.

4. Embryo rescue

Wide tomatoes possess rare genes that enable them to survive diseases and resist insects without the help of pesticides and thrive in poor soils. This makes them useful breeding materials, and is being exploited for resistance to fruitworm, bacterial wilt, black leaf mold, and late blight. But it is difficult to cross a certain wide tomato with a cultivated variety because of differences in genetic constitution. Cross-fertilization can occur, but the embryo seldom survives. This phenomenon prevents the transfer into cultivated tomato of many useful traits, such as resistance to tomato yellow leaf curl virus. Tissue culture makes it possible to rescue wide-cross embryos that contain desirable genes and maintain them through several cycles of backcross.

The wide-cross seeds cannot survive like ordinary seeds. They must be harvested two weeks after fertilization and their embryos removed under sterile conditions in the laboratory. The "rescued" embryos are cultured in test tube until they germinate. When plantlets are green and have developed root systems, they are transferred in a controlled environment. Only when they have begun to grow vigorously are they transferred to soil. The rescued plant is then cross back to its cultivated parent until it attains the desired characteristics and regain fertility. In 1994, genes for resistance to Taiwan tomato leaf curl virus, the local geminivirus strain, were successfully incorporated into three AVRDC improved tomato lines from Lycopersicon chiiense, a wide tomato from Chile, using this technique. This technique is highly significant in intractable and long duration horticultural species. Many of the dry land legume species have been successfully regenerated

from cotyledons, hypocotyls, leaf, ovary, protoplast, petiole root, anthers, etc., Haploid generation through anther/pollen culture is recognized as another important area in crop improvement. It is useful in being rapid and economically feasible.

Hybrids in legume species obtained through embryo and ovule culture between naturally incompatible species

Glycine max   x *G. tomentella*
Phaseolus coccineus x *Phaseolus* spp.
Phaseolus vulgaris x *Phaseolus* spp.

Complete homozygosity of the offspring helps in phenotype selection for quantitative characters and particularly for qualitatively inherited characters making breeding much easier successful isolation, culture and fusion of plant protoplasts has been very useful in transferring cytoplasmic male sterility for obtaining hybrid vigour through mitochondrial recombination and for genetic transformation in plants.

Some example of somatic embryogenesis in vegetables

Carrot	-	Root
Potato	-	Hypocotyl
Pumpkin	-	Cotyledons
Cucumber	-	Anthers (Somatic tissue)

5. Mutation

Gamma radiation at the dose of 15 Gy can be successfully applied in vitro as a mutagenic factor in chrysanthemum breeding. Induced mutagenesis is very effective chrysanthemum breeding method, as confirmed in the past by many other authors. New chrysanthemum cultivars were obtained by using single-node explants from irradiated micro cuttings or by irradiating leaf explants with callus regenerated earlier on leaf petiole. Quantitative and qualitative changes in the content of pigments in inflorescences of the cultivars obtained were a result of mutagenic gamma radiation (Rumiska 2004).

In vitro germplasm conservation is of great significance in providing solutions and alternative approaches to overcoming constrains in management of genetic resources. In crops which are propagated vegetatively and which produce recalcitrant seeds and perennial crops which are highly heterozygous seed storage is not suitable. In such crops especially, *in vitro* storage is of great practical importance. These techniques have successfully been demonstrated in a number of

horticultural crops and there are now various germplasm collection centers. *In vitro* germplasm also assures the exchange of pest and disease free material and helps in better quarantine.

Herbicide tolerance: Transgenic plants are developed that are resistant to herbicides allowing farmers to spray crops so as to kill only weeds but not their crops. Many herbicide tolerant plants have been developed in tomato, tobacco, potato, soybean, cotton, corn oilseed rape, petunia, etc. Glyphosate is one of the most potent broad spectrum environment friendly herbicide known, it is marketed under the trade name Round up. Glyphosate kills plants by blocking the action of an enzyme (5-enolpyruvyl shikimate-3-phosphate synthase) (EPSPS) an essential enzyme in the biosynthesis of aromatic amino acids, tyrosine, phenylalanine and tryptophan.

Amino acids are building blocks of protein. Transgenic plants resistant to Glyphosate have been developed by transferring gene of EPSPS that over produce this enzyme thus inhibiting the effect of Glyphosate. A number of detoxifying enzymes have been identified in plants as well as in microbes. Some of these include glutahthione-s-transferase or GST in maize and other plants which detoxifies the herbicide bromoxynil and phosphinothricin acetyl transferase (PAT) which detoxifies the herbicide PPT (L-phosphinothricine).

Transgenic plants using *bxn* gene from Klebsiella and *bar* gene from *Streptomyces* have been obtained in potato, oilseed, sugarbeet, soybean, cotton and corn and are found to be herbicide resistance.

6. Engineering Pathogen Resistance

Viruses are the major pests of crop plants which cause considerable yield losses. Many strategies have been applied to control virus infection using coat protein and satellite RNA. Viruses are sub-microscopic pockets of nucleic acid (DNA or RNA) enclosed in a protein coat and can multiply within a host cell. Use of viral coat protein as a transgene for producing virus resistant plants is one of the most spectacular successes achieved in plant biotechnology. Coat protein gene from tobacco mosaic virus (TMV) classified as a positive strand RNA virus has been transferred to tobacco, making it nearly resistant against TMV.

Using gene for resistance has been introduced in crops like tomato, tobacco, lettuce, groundnut, pepper and in ornaments like *Impatiens*, *Ageratum* and *Crysnathemum* against tomato spotted wilt virus. Use of satellite RNA (SATRNA) makes many transgenic plants resistant to Cucumber Mosaic Virus (CMV). Transgenic resistant plants have also been developed against alfalfa mosaic

virus, potato virus X, Rice tungro virus, tobacco rattle virus and Papaya ring spot virus.

During the last decade many resistance genes whose products are involved in recognizing the invading pathogens have been identified and cloned. A number of signaling pathways which follow the pathogen infection have been dissected. Many of the antifungal compounds synthesized by plants which combat fungal infections have been identified. The major strategies for developing fungal resistance have been production of transgenic plants with antifungal molecules like proteins and toxins, and generation of hypersensitive response through R genes or by manipulating genes of SAR pathway. A chitinase gene from bean plants in tobacco and *Brassica napus* showed enhanced resistance to *Rhizoctonia solani*. In another case chitinase gene obtained from *Serratia marcescens* (soil bacterium) is introduced in tobacco making it resistant to *Alternaria longipes* which causes brown spot diseases. Acetyl transferase gene is introduced in tobacco making it resistant to *Pseudomonas syringea*, a causal agent of wild fire disease.

7. Stress Resistance

A number of genes responsible for providing resistance against stresses such as to water stress heat, cold, salt, heavy metals and phytohormones have been identified. Studies are also being conducted on metabolites like proteins and betains that have been implicated in stress tolerance. Resistance against chilling was introduced into tobacco plants by introducing gene for glycerol-1-phosphate acyl-transferase enzyme from *Arabidopsis*. Many plants respond to drought stress by synthesizing a group of sugar derivatives called polyols (Mannitol, Sorbitol and Sion). Plants that have more polyols are more resistant to stress. Using a bacterial gene capable of synthesizing mannitols it is possible to raise the level of mannitol very high making plants resistant to drought.

8. Fruit Quality

Tomatoes which ripen slowly are helpful in transportation process. Transgenic tomato with reduced pectin methyl esterase activity and increased level of soluble solids and higher pH increases processing quality. Tomatoes exhibiting delayed ripening have been produced either by using antisense RNA against enzymes involved in ethylene production (Eg ACC synthase) or by using gene for deaminase which degraded 1-aminocyclopropane-1-carboxylic acid (ACC) an immediate precursor of ethylene. This increases the shelf-life of tomatoes. These tomatoes can also stay on the plant long giving more time for accumulation of sugars and acids for improving flavour. It is produced at

commercial level in European and American countries. Tomatoes with elevated sucrose and reduced starch could also be produced using sucrose phosphate synthase gene. Starch content in potatoes has been increased by 20-40% by using a bacterial ADP glucose pyrophosphorylase gene.

9. Pest Resistance

The insecticidal beta endotoxin gene (bt gene) has been isolated from *Bacillus thuringiensis* the commonly occurring soil bacteria and transferred to number of plants like cotton, tobacco, tomato, soybean, potato, etc. to make them resistant to attack by insects. These genes produce insecticidal crystal proteins which affect a range of lepidopteran, coleopteran, dipteran insects. These crystals upon ingestion by the insect larva are solubilised in the highly alkaline midgut into individual protoxins which vary from 133 to 136 kDa in molecular weight. Insecticidal crystal protein produced during vegetative growth of the cells (VIP) are also found to be highly effective against insect control. Bt resistant plants are already in the market.

10. Male sterility and Fertility restoration

This is helpful in hybrid seed production. Transgenic plants with male sterility and fertility restoration genes have become available in *Brassica napus*. It facilitates production of hybrid seed without manual emasculation and controlled pollination as often done in maize. In 1990, Mariani and others from Belgium have successfully used a gene construct having another specific promoter from TA29 gene of tobacco and bacterial coding sequence for a ribonuclease gene from Bacillus Sp. (barnase gene) for production of transgenic plants in *Brassica napus*. Here the translated gene prevented normal pollen development leading to male sterility.

Plant breeders are continually searching for new genetic variability that is potentially useful in cultivar improvement. A portion of plants regenerated by tissue culture often exhibits phenotypic variation atypical of the original phenotype. Such variation, termed somaclonal variation may be heritable i.e. genetically stable and passed on to the next generation. Alternatively, the variation may be epigenetic and disappear following sexual reproduction. These heritable variation are potentially useful to plant breeders.

Biotechnology has been applied to improving the sensory properties and shelf life of vegetables. Some of the innovations, particularly in texture or flavor enhancement, have not been highly publicized as originating from plants modified by methods included in a broad definition of biotechnology. These include carrot, potato, celery, pepper, and melon varieties improved through applications of tissue culture. Public awareness of developments in agricultural biotechnology is primarily

associated with genetic engineering, particularly of tomato. In 1994, the first genetically engineered food product reached consumer markets. Calgene's Flavr Savr tomato received widespread publicity during development and commercial introduction. The targeted benefit, shared by several companies developing new tomato varieties, was to deliver to the market tomatoes with improved flavor and reduced rates of softening or decay.

11. Reference

1) Koundal, K.R. (2004). Biotechnology - A modern tool for crop improvement in horticulture. Acta Horti. 662: 307 - 309.
2) Rumiska J., Zalewska M. (2004). Studies on flower pigment of Chrysanthemum mutants: Nero and Wonder Groups. Acta Sci. Pol., Hortorum Cultus 3(1): 125 -135.
3) Singh B.D. 2006. Plant Biotechnology. Kalyani Publication. New Delhi.

Scientific Advancements in Current Agricultural Research
ISBN: 978-81-947154-7-4
First Edition; 2020
Chapter – 9, Page: 90 - 94

9

ROOFTOP GARDENING - A BOON FOR GREENING INDIA

C. Muruganandam[1], T. Uma Maheswari[1] and V. Velmurugan[2*]

[1]Department of Horticulture, Faculty of Agriculture, Annamalai University, Annamalai Nagar, Tamil Nadu, India
[2]Management Wing, DDE, Annamalai University, Annamalai Nagar, Tamil Nadu, India.

Abstract

Rooftop garden is a garden that cultivates vegetables, fruits or flowers on the terrace, balconies or roof of buildings, also called as a terrace garden. The kitchen garden, a standard in every Indian household, has shifted to the roof due to constraints of space, and called a terrace garden. Besides decorative benefit, roof plantings may provide fresh horticultural produce, temperature control, hydrological benefits, architectural enhancement, habitats or corridor for wildlife, and recreational opportunities. Establishing a roof top garden is eco-friendly and thus can reduce temperatures by 4-5°C thus reducing the cooler and air-conditioners utility. Roof gardening industry can be effective in masking the paucity in vegetable availability in populous nations like India.

Key words: Roof top garden, Terrace garden and Green roofs.

1. Introduction

Roof top garden is a garden that cultivates vegetables, fruits or flowers on the terrace, balconies or roof of buildings, also called as a terrace garden. The kitchen garden, a standard in every Indian household, has shifted to the roof due to constraints of space, and called a terrace garden. Besides decorative benefit, roof plantings may provide fresh horticultural produce, temperature control, hydrological benefits, architectural enhancement, habitats or corridor for wildlife, and recreational

opportunities. Establishing a roof top garden is eco-friendly and thus can reduce temperatures by 4 – 5 °C thus reducing the cooler and air-conditioners utility. Roof gardening industry can be effective in masking the paucity in vegetable availability in populous nations like India. A roof garden also helps make the building naturally aesthetic.

Rooftops are one of our cities' greatest untapped resources. They account for hundreds of acres of empty, under-utilized space, contributing to problems like the "heat island effect" and increased storm-water run-off. But rooftops could easily be turned into valuable green spaces, by creating green roofs of wildflowers, trees and shrubs or vegetables on schools, apartments, homes and places of work throughout the city. Green roofs and rooftop gardens can provide many benefits, including:

- Increased access to safe outdoor green space;
- Avenue for urban food production;
- Promotion of individual, community and cultural diversity;
- Areas for study and horticultural therapy;
- Improved air quality and absorption of carbon dioxide;
- Minimization of storm water run-off, and support for a rainwater collection system;
- Increased habitat for birds, butterflies and insects; and
- Reduced heating and cooling costs by providing a layer of insulation on buildings.

No much technology and modern briefings are required for establishing a terrace garden except for PVC coated roof top and can be followed as a hobby by many garden amateurs. Much of the shallow rooted crops can be easily grown above the roof tops while utilizing the runoffs, filtered sewage discharges and organic kitchen wastes. Thus roof gardening can be shortcut for urban greening any nation well in advance while increasing horticultural yield. These gardens can be created on almost all kinds of buildings like residential flats, individual houses, commercial hubs, godowns and factories. Plants with fibrous roots do not cause any harm to the roof but avoid tap roots as they can penetrate the roof and harm it by growing its roots in the structure.

The concept that makes the roofing material green, or environmentally friendly, is not just the raw materials it comes from and how it is manufactured; it's also how the roof performs over its lifetime and how the roofing is disposed of at the end of its life. The key performance factors are overall durability and the material's resistance to heat gain, which can affect the cost of cooling the home. The Energy

Chapter - 9

Star program certifies a number of roofing materials for relatively high heat reflectivity, or their ability to reflect heat away from the roof, thus lowering cooling costs. Energy Star certification is not limited to specific roofing materials (Murrye Bernard, 2020).

2. Loading capacity

Typically, roofs are designed for a combined load of 40 pounds per square foot. Wet soil weighs 100 pounds per cubic foot, so six inches of soil across a roof would add a load of 45 to 63 pounds per square foot. Soil should be mixed with organic and inorganic matter to lighten its weight, or use light weight growing mediums, such as pre-mixed planting soils found at your local garden centre (typically a combination of peat moss, compost or other organic matter, and vermiculite or perlite).

3. Water proofing

A completely new waterproofing system should be installed to protect the building's structure. There are several types of waterproofing available; however, elastomeric materials offer the greatest protection. Bituminous waterproofing should be avoided. Over time the organic components in bituminous waterproofing interact with the soils and the plant materials and therefore increase the likelihood of system failure. A properly installed waterproofing system can last the lifetime of the building, however a single small leak may require the removal of the entire garden to find and repair the damage. Therefore, in order to insure the integrity of the waterproofing it is recommended a protective topping coat of concrete be applied, as soon as possible, following the installation of the new waterproofing.

4. Drainage

Keeping access to the drainage system free and clear is a priority. This can be done on green roofs   by maintaining a gravel ring and filter cloth layer around roof drains and overflow scuppers. On rooftop gardens, it should be ensured that any deck strapping or containers are aligned in such a way that they don't block the flow of water to the drain or eaves trough. It is essential to watch and determine where water flows onto roof and it should be ensured that those areas and drainage paths are maintained.

The drainage layer, directly above the concrete protective slab, should be very porous to permit water to pass easily through it. It must be permanent and continuous over the entire roof surface and strong enough to support the weight of the plant materials and hardscape above it. This layer must be kept free of any materials that could prevent the free flow of water to the drains.

5. Containers

The easiest and most personal approach to rooftop gardening is the use of containers and raised beds. Containers of all sizes, shapes, whether of plastic, ceramic, metal or mud can be used. Even coke bottles, take away plastic boxes, old sacks, coconut shells, old broken buckets, dented kitchen pots and pans , just about everything can be recycled and used as containers.

6. Crops

Vegetables like coriander, fenugreek, gram, drumsticks, tomatoes and chilli and even fruit trees like banana, lime and pomegranate can be grown. At least 6 vegetables per season can be grown. And 1 sqm of terrace area can give anywhere between 25 to 50 kg of vegetables in a year.

7. Shade net

Indian summers can be scorching. As much as plants love the sunshine, too much of it can wilt the plants, if not kill them. It is better to buy a shade or reuse an old mosquito net to protect container plants from excessive heat and torrential rains.

8. Support

If it is a vegetable garden, it is better to have a trellis for climbers and creepers to grow comfortably. Wooden poles; PVC pipes or bamboo sticks can also be used to create a square or rectangular support for the plants.

9. Media

Soil is another one of the primary elements needed for a terrace garden. The soil must be enriched with all the necessary nutrients needed for plant growth. Sand, coco peat and compost can be mixed in equal parts to create ideal soil. Some plants must be transplanted to another pot if they are to yield a good produce.

10. Seed trays

If transplanted vegetables are grown, it is necessary to sow the seeds in one container and when they germinate and sprout a few leaves, it is to be transferred to the primary pot where it is planned to be grown. Seed trays come in very handy for this purpose. Cardboard boxes, citrus peels, egg shells and curd/yogurt cups can also be used to sow the seeds as our own creativity.

11. Irrigation

The relatively thin, well-drained soil mixtures used in roof garden construction cannot provide the plantings with the subsurface water normally

available to ground level plantings. Care must be exercised to prevent the soil mass from drying out and causing damage to the plant materials. Hand watering is too labor intensive and is not cost effective. Drip irrigation is preferred in roof garden applications because the effects of wind can cause above ground systems to perform inconsistently.

12. Mulch

Drying and overheating of the soil can be prevented by the application of 2-3 inches of shredded hardwood mulch. Besides providing protection of the plant materials this mulch serves to hide the drip irrigation lines and emitters.

13. Maintenance

To maintain clear access to the roofing membrane and drains for maintenance and repair, it is needed to install rooftop garden in sections. This can easily be done using containers of any height or size, arranged in sections on roof. Designing rooftop garden in sections will avoid removing the entire garden area each time the roof needs some repair work.

14. Cost

Establishing roof top garden is based on the cost that we are going to spend. We can start small and add on, buying more pots and plants (and soil). The real expense comes when we want to start hardscaping and building on the roof. Laying tiles or stone, building raised beds and boxes, adding lighting and furniture can all start to add up and, more structural work is needed to support them (Marie Iannotti, 2020).

15. Conclusion

Irrespective of design, a rooftop garden is an investment in peace of mind for many urban dwellers, providing hours of relaxation and reward. Thus, roof top garden converts CO_2 emissions. It produces oxygen. It reduces the heat of buildings and energy costs. It creates a habitat for wildlife. It reduces ambient temperature. It captures and harvests rainwater and It reduces storm water runoff and discharge.

16. Reference

1) Marie Iannotti, 2020. Rooftop gardening. The spruce. www.thespruce.com/rooftop-gardening-1403340
2) Murrye Bernard. 2020. Sustainable Roofing Materials: What to Know. The spruce. https://www.thespruce.com/sustainable-roofing-materials-1821784.

Scientific Advancements in Current Agricultural Research
ISBN: 978-81-947154-7-4
First Edition; 2020
Chapter – 10, Page: 95 - 110

10

RECENT TRENDS IN VALUE ADDITION OF TROPICAL FRUIT CROPS

T. Uma Maheswari[*], S. Sinduja, S. Kamalakannan and J. Padmanaban

Department of Horticulture, Faculty of Agriculture, Annamalai University, Annamalai Nagar, Tamil Nadu, India
*Corresponding author: umahorti2003@gmail.com

Abstract

Fruits are being a highly perishable, it suffers from high postharvest losses to the extent of about 30 to 40 %. Among the several techniques available for preservation of fruits and dehydration is also widely adopted for preservation. The processing of fruit industry improves the capabilities of rural communities to increase their productivity, access more lucrative markets and obtain shares in marketing and processing activities as a means of obtaining larger share of the value in the chain. Tropical fruits like mango, banana, citrus, guava, sapota, papaya, jackfruit is rich in vitamins, minerals, nutritional and medicinal values. Therefore, it is necessary to convert fresh produce to value added product that can retain color, flavor and nutrients provided with extended shelf life. The value-added products made from the fruits are jam, jelly, juice, pickle, flour, powder, chocolate, cheese, butter, biscuit, ice-cream, pulp, squash, candy, osmo-dehydrated product, bar, tooty-fruity, nectar, chewing gum, slices, milkshake and bread ect., This study deals with the products made from the tropical fruit crops and their preservation.

Key words: Value addition, Fruit crops and Preservation.

1. Introduction

Value-added products are defined by USDA as having: A change in the physical state or form of the product (such as milling wheat into flour or making strawberries into jam). The production of a product in a manner that enhances its value such as organically produced products. It is adding value to a raw product by taking it into, at least the next stage of production.

2. Production and Export of Value-added Fruit Crops

In India, the total fruit production is about 98 MT (Statista, 2020). It has been estimated that 40 % of fruits are wasted before consumption due to post harvest losses. The global export of the fruit product is less than 1.0 % (APEDA, 2020).

3. Why Value addition is important?

- Processing of fruits into value added products is one of the strategies to reduce postharvest losses and promote consumption of fruits.
- For better income.
- To provide variety of products
- To improve profitability of farmers and to reduce economic risk of marketing
- To provide better quality, safe and branded foods.
- Preparation of Value-Added Products Through Preservation.
- Fruits and vegetables provide an abundant and inexpensive source of energy, body-building nutrients, vitamins, and minerals.
- However, most fruits and vegetables are only edible for a very short time unless they are promptly and properly preserved.

The stage of crop production immediately following harvest, including cooling, cleaning, sorting and packing may be termed as Post Harvest Handling. Fresh Fruits and Vegetables including root crops are mostly perishable in nature. They begin to deteriorate immediately after its separation from the parent plant and suffer considerable losses during the process of Marketing. These losses may be of following nature

- Quality downgrading due to handling
- Physiological spoilage (rooting & sprouting)
- Pathological Spoilage from pest and diseases
- Oversupply to markets

4. Main Reason of Post-Harvest Losses

- Inadequate or inappropriate application of proper Post Harvest Practices.
- Improper production planning.

On the Other hand, Value Addition in Horticulture is the process in which a high price is realized for the same volume of a primary product, by means of processing, packing, upgrading the quality or other such methods. For example: Making Jam of Pomegranate and Strawberry.

5. Need for value addition in Horticulture

- To improve the profitability of farmers.
- To empower the farmers and other weaker sections of society especially women through gainful employment opportunities and revitalize rural communities.
- To provide better quality, safe and branded foods to the consumers.
- To emphasize primary and secondary processing.
- To reduce post-harvest losses.
- Reduction of import and meeting export demands.
- Way of increased foreign exchange.
- Encourage growth of subsidiary industries.
- Reduce the economic risk of marketing.
- Increase opportunities for smaller farms and companies through the development of markets.
- Diversify the economic base of rural communities.
- Overall, increase farmers' financial stability.

6. Scope and Importance of Value Addition in Horticulture

Horticulture deals a large group of crops having great medicinal, nutritional, health promoting values. India as second largest producer of fruits and vegetables, only 10 per cent of that horticultural produce is processed, but other developed and developing countries where 40 - 80 per cent produce is value added. Horticultural crops provide varied type of components, which can be effectively and gainfully utilized for value addition like pigment, amino acids, oleoresins, antioxidants, flavors, aroma etc. Post-harvest losses in horticultural produce are 5 to 30 per cent which amounts to more than 8000 crore rupees per annum. If we subject our produce to value addition the losses can be checked. Horticultural crops are right material for

value addition because they are more profitable, has high degree of process ability and richness in health promoting compounds and higher potential for export.

8. Banana

The fruit banana, is produced on a large scale in the country. Banana is consumed as fresh and also in processed forms such as figs, snack foods and chips. But being highly perishable in nature, there is a strong need to minimize the huge post -harvest losses of this important fruit.

Preparation of Banana Bread to utilize the Over Ripe Banana

The main aim of preparation of banana bread is to utilize the over ripe banana in form of banana bread which increases the appetite of body, because of the fried, baked or dried banana. The cooked banana reduces the chances of cough and cold as compare to the raw banana. Banana bread helps to stabilize blood sugar level as well as cholesterol level. Also it improves the digestive health. Bread was prepared using flour, sugar, salt, water, yeast along with fats and emulsifier were mixed together to form a dough. The dough was kneaded till clean up stage and allowed to ferment for two and a half hours. Then the dough was divided into dough ball, moulded placed in furnace at 350 – 400 °C for 30 - 40 minutes. The banana bread was successfully developed by considering the physio-chemical and sensory evaluation. From the analysis of physico-chemical properties and sensory analysis evaluation, the sample B was found better than other sample with physical value 15 cm length, 5 cm width & 8 cm thickness, chemical value 5 g/100 g protein, 9.7 g/100 g carbohydrate & 2 g/100 g fat and sensory value on hedonic scale having color, taste, flavor, texture and appearance & overall acceptability (Minali Masih and Tushar Desalein, 2019).

Utilization of Banana in the development of Nutrient Rich Banana Bar

The suitable variety of bananas is collected from the nearby market, just before processing. The bananas are hygienically peeled in the aseptic conditions. Proper measures are to be taken to avoid damage, to the bananas and to prevent the browning reactions immediately. After peeling the bananas are immediately blanched, at a temperature of 85 °C, for about 5 minutes. Immediate blanching prevents the rapid enzymatic browning, and inactivates the polyphenoloxidase, which is responsible for the browning reactions. For blanching, we have to use clean and soft water for blanching. Blanched slices are thoroughly mashed, in a mixer and strained to extract the pulp. Citric acid and KMS are added to the pulp, by dissolving in a table spoon of water. After the pulp is ready, suitable plates are selected and smeared with glycerin or butter. After smearing, the pulp is spread uniformly in the

plates. These are kept for drying, which is completed at about 550 °C for about 10 - 12 hours. After drying the banana slabs, they are cut into good looking pieces and are wrapped in polythene covers and are stored in an air tight container. Organoleptic testing, by a 5 points hedonic scale is found that, samples T3 & T2 are ideal in taste, texture and over all acceptability. The other samples are found to be crystallized and undergone through browning, for further studies. Banana bar is an instant energy producing bar which provides a good mouth feel. It can be used as snack item. It has health benefits like decreasing blood pressure, soothes ulcer and also provides good energy value (Aruna *et al.,* 2017).

9. Mango

Preparation of Mango Kernel Flour

Evenly ripened disease free and sound mango fruits have been selected. The pulp and seed of mango fruit was separated manually. Mango seeds were washed and dried in hot air at 60 °C for 6 hours. Kernels were separated from stone manually using stainless steel knife and dried in hot air oven at 50 °C for 4 hours and stored in air tight containers. During processing stored kernels were soaked (18 - 20 hrs) in water, chopped into small pieces, blanched (1 - 2 min), dried (60 °C for 5 hours) and ground into flour in electric blender, sieved and stored in air tight container.

Preparation of Biscuits

First dry ingredients were sieved and mixed together. Sugar and fat were creamed together. Soft dough was prepared in dough mixer with all the ingredients and an adequate amount of water. Dough was spread into a sheet and cut into suitable shapes and size. Cut pieces were gently placed on baking tray. Tray was placed in oven for approximately 15 minutes at 170 °C. Baked biscuits were removed from oven and cooled. Prepared Biscuits were packed in suitable packaging material.

Mango kernel flour replaced the wheat flour to the extent of 0 %, 10 %, 20 %, 30 % and 40 % levels without altering the total flour content of the preparation. The variety selected in this study is locally available Kesar Mango. Mango stone was separated and processed to prepare Mango kernel flour. Biscuits were formulated from refined wheat flour incorporated with Mango kernel flour. Based on sensory evaluation biscuit sample was selected. The addition of 30 per cent Mango kernel flour yielded a nutritious product with nutraceutical properties with good sensory attributes.

Chapter – 10

Preparation and evaluation of Fruit Candy from Unripe Mango

This experiment was conducted by Mahato and his co-workers in the year 2019 at Bidhan Chandra Krishi Viswavidyalaya, Mohanpur, Nadia, West Bengal, India.

Preparation of Candy

The laboratory work was carried out with eight treatments comprising three replications *viz.*, Hot water blanching + Powder sugar (T1), Steam Blanching + powder sugar (T2), Steam Blanching + 400 Brix sugar syrup (T3), Without blanching + powder sugar (T4), Hot water blanching + honey (T5), Steam blanching + honey (T6), Hot water blanching + 400 Brix honey syrup (T7) and Without blanching + honey (T8). The fruits were peeled off and cut into small cubes in uniform size then mango cubes were blanched in boiling water at 98 ± 2 °C or in steam for 2 - 5 minutes. After that mango cubes are added in the sugar after impregnating overnight, mango pieces were separated from solution and the TSS of the drained syrup was increased by heating the syrup or adding some sugar or honey upto 600 Brix and kept for overnight. Next day the TSS was increased upto 70^0 Brix and then 75° Brix on 4th day respectively. The mango pieces were removed from the concentrated syrup after that, those pieces were dried by keeping it at room temperature under the ceiling fan for four hours and then packed in the polythene bags. The mean data of overall acceptability of mango candy as influenced by blanching method, methods of sugar and honey addition and their interactions. Treatment T3 and T7 exhibited highest overall acceptance during entire period of storage. Treatment as compared to flavor, taste and general appearance are important consideration of overall acceptance of the product. That the T3 treatment helped in maintaining the color, taste, texture and flavor of the product during storage, which ultimately resulted in higher overall acceptance score up to 180 day of storage.

10. Physico-chemical and Rheological study of Orange pulp fortified Cookies

This study was conducted by Haque and his co-workers in the year 2015 at Ayub Agriculture Research Institute, Faislabad, Pakistan. This study was aimed to find out the effects of supplementation of wheat cookies with orange pulp fiber at 0 %, 3 %, 6 % and 9 % levels.

Preparation of Orange pulp powder

Citrus pulp powder was prepared according to the method reported by Fernandez-Lopez *et al.* (2018). Oranges were washed with warm water to remove possible pathogenic microorganisms (vegetative cells). Afterwards, oranges were pressed using a helical press to remove excess liquid prior to drying. Drying was

carried out in an oven at 50 °C for 24 hrs. A grinder mill and sieves were used to obtain a powder with the particle size of less than 0.2 mm.

Development of Cookies

Cookies were prepared in Cereal Research Institute, Ayub Agriculture Faisalabad, Pakistan according to Approved Methods of American Association of Cereal Chemists (AACC), method no. 10-50D with some modifications. The orange pulp powder was added at the rate of 0, 3, 6and 9 % along with other ingredients.

The use of orange pulp fiber in cookies has the advantage of improving the fiber, ash and phytochemical levels in cookies. However, only cookies produced with 6% orange pulp fiber had acceptable sensory quality. With increasing levels of orange pulp fiber, the sensory characteristics of cookies were affected badly. The results indicate that orange pulp fiber a by-product from orange processing, could be considered as an alternative dietary fiber for cookies and other bakery products.

11. Preparation of Candy from Kinnow (*Citrus* sp.) peel

This study was conducted by Bhatlu and his co-workers in the year 2014 at Institute of Agricultural Sciences, BHU, Varanasi, U.P, India. In this study, we are preparing candy from kinnow peel. This will not only reduce the waste but also add value to citrus fruit.

Preparation of Candy

The peels were cut uniformly about 1cm of length and breadth. The thickness of the peels was maintained to 1mm using scraper. Then some small pores were made in the peels for the proper insertion of sugar syrup into the peels. The Kinnow peel candy was made under three different sugar syrup concentrations viz. 40 °Brix, 50 °Brix and 60 °Brix. The peels were dipped in the sugar syrup with constant cooking and stirring gently. After proper cooking the candies were taken out of the pan or vessels used and were dried. It was observed that candy prepared in the maximum sugar concentration (60 °B).

Three different samples of kinnow peel under three different treatments (50 °C for 15 minutes cooked in 40 oBrix sugar syrup solution, 60 °Cfor 20 minutes cooked in 50 oBrix sugar syrup solution and 70 °Cfor 25 minutes in 60 oBrix sugar syrup solution) have been prepared. All the samples were tested on the basis of hedonic scale tested on a panel of 7 experts. Sample 1 has acceptable color but it gives a raw peel type off-flavor in mouth after eating. Sample 2 was also quite acceptable with respect to color and taste. But sample 3 gives the best result among all the three

samples. It gives chocolate color to the kinnow peel candy probably due to caramelization of sugar. The candy completely look likes a chocolate.

12. Sapota

Sapota is one among the highly perishable fruit and hence marketing the fresh fruits to different places is quite very difficult. Therefore, it is necessary to convert the fresh produce into a value added product that can retain color, flavor and nutrients provided with extended shelf life.

Development of Intermediate Moisture Sapota slices by Osmotic Dehydration

This study was conducted by G. Gurumeenakshi and R. Rajeswari in the year 2020 at Tamil Nadu Agricultural University, Coimbatore, Tamil Nadu, India. This research work was undertaken to study the different pretreatment processing on the quality attributes of osmo dried sapota slices. Ripened sapota of uniform size and color with firm texture from widely grown variety of sapota (PKM 1 [V1] and cricket ball variety [V2]) was selected for the osmotic dehydration experiment using food grade sugar as an osmotic agent.

Preparation of Osmo Dried Sapota

Selected fruits were thoroughly washed under tap water before slicing to remove adhering impurities. The outer skin of the fruit was carefully peeled off manually using sharp stainless steel knife without damaging the pulp, destoned and cut into slices (6 x 2 cm). The fruit slices (1000 g) were soaked for 30 minutes in citric acid (0.5 %) + sodium benzoate (0.5 %)/ascorbic acid solutions (0.5 %) + sodium benzoate (0.5 %) (1000 ml) respectively. The fruit slices that were not given any pretreatment served as control. The treated and control fruit slices were soaked in the osmotic agent separately. The fruit slices (1 kg) to osmotic agent (1litre) ratio were 1:1 During the process of osmosis three levels of concentration (40, 50 and 60o Brix) and temperature of the osmotic agent were maintained at 60 °C by placing them in the water bath for the first two hours to facilitate effective osmosis. The sugar syrup was stirred manually at regular intervals in order to maintain uniform temperature. The fruit slices were then allowed to remain in the osmotic agent for a period of 16 hrs for effective osmosis to take place. After 16 hrs, the sugar syrup was drained and the fruit slices were arranged in trays and dried in a cabinet drier at a temperature of 60 °C for 6 hrs. The product after dehydration was cooled and packed in metalized polypropylene packs.

The study concluded that PKM1 variety of sapota is more suitable for osmotic dehydration than cricket ball variety. The best pretreatment for osmotic dehydration of sapota was found to be ascorbic acid than citric acid at it retains the

Chapter – 10

nutritional properties of the sapota during storage. The product that of ascorbic acid treated sapota (PKM1 variety) had highest score for sensory attributes of appearance, color, flavor and overall acceptability. The unit cost of osmo dried sapota slices (10g) was Rs. 1.85, which was cheaper than sugar boiled confectioneries and chocolates.

Preparation and preservation of Sapota Juice

This experiment was conducted by Hiremath and Rokhadein the year 2012 at Department of Post-Harvest Technology, K.R.C.C.H. Arabhavi. The investigation on processing of sapota fruits was carried out in the Department of Post-harvest Technology, Kittur Rani Channamma College of Horticulture, Arabhavi, district Belgaum, Karnataka during the year 2005 - 2006. Kalipatti, a commercially important cultivar of this region was used for the study.

The design of the experiment was Completely Randomized Design (CRD) with nine treatments and three replications. Fruits of uniform colour, size and shape were selected. Diseased and damaged ones were discarded. Fruits were washed in clean tap water and hand peeled with the help of stainless steel knife. Seeds and core were separated. The pulp was chopped into small pieces and squeezed in double layered muslin cloth to obtain juice. As per the treatments, the juice was pasteurized separately either at 60 °C or 65 °C for 10 minutes and cooled immediately. In case of treatments T4 and T5, sodium benzoate and in T7 and T8, potassium metabisulphite was added at the rate of 700 and 600 ppm, respectively. In treatments T3 and T6, sodium benzoate (700 ppm) and potassium metabisulphite (600 ppm) were added respectively, to the extracted juice (without pasteurization). In case of T1 and T2, no preservative was added to the pasteurized juice. The juices treated as per the treatments were filled in to clean, sterilized crown bottles of 200 ml capacity, sealed with crown caps using crown corking machine and stored at ambient condition.

The scores with respect to colour and appearance of sapota juice indicated significant differences between the treatments. Among the treatments, T6 recorded highest score of 5 followed by T3 and T9 (4.75), whereas significantly lowest score was observed in T1 and T8 (4.25). Significantly highest score for taste was observed in T9 (4.80) followed by T6 (4.75). The treatments T5 and T8 recorded significantly lowest score (4.40) for taste. Significantly highest score for flavour was observed for T9 (4.90) followed by T3 and T6 (4.75), whereas the lowest score was recorded in T5 (4.40). The treatment T9 (4.75) recorded significantly highest score for overall acceptability, whereas lowest was recorded in T5 (4.40).

13. Value addition of Guava Cheese cv. Allahabad Safeda by Medicinal Herbs

This experiment was conducted by Sinha and co-workers in the year 2017 at Department of Horticulture, SHUATS, Allahabad, Uttar Pradesh, India. Guava cheese would ensure the consumer benefits of guava along with its delightful taste of cheese. In this study, the beneficial property of this fruit was enhanced to create a value added product along with ginger powder, lemon grass extract and ashwagandha powder (0.5 %, 1.0 % and 1.5 % concentration)

Method of Guava Cheese

Fresh guava fruits were washed, cut into pieces and boil with equal quantity of water. Scum and pomace was removed by sieving and added sugar (700 g/kg of pulp), butter (90 g/kg of pulp), citric acid (2 g/kg of pulp) and value additives (0.5 g, 1.0 g and 1.5 g/kg Ginger powder, Lemon grass extract and Ashwagandha powder) per kg guava pulp cooked till, until mixture become sufficiently thick, and then after removed from fire when mixture starts leaving side of the pan evenly distributed over butter coated tray and left for 3 hours to set cut into pieces, with a sharp.

Ingredients	Quantity
Sugar	750 g/kg of pulp
Butter	90 g/kg of pulp
Citric acid	2g/kg of pulp
Value additive product for guava cheese	Ratio of 0.5, 1.0, 1.5 % of medicinal herbs (ginger, lemon grass & ashwagandha)

Based on above study with value added guava cheese, most of the treatments showed acceptable results. It was observed that T0 showed minimum loss in physiological weight of storage, minimum pH, TSS, high reducing and total sugar percentage. T9 showed a higher ascorbic acid during the storage period. T9 have all the desirable qualities and is having most overall acceptability throughout the storage period. By far, it can be concluded that T9 (Guava cheese + Ashwagandha @ 1.5 %) is the best Value added product as for the overall acceptability and physicochemical properties and it can be standardized in commercial scale. Moreover, the cost benefit ratio of T9 (Guava cheese + Ashwagandha @ 1.5 %) was also found maximum. Hence, it could be suggested that T9 (Guava cheese + Ashwagandha @1.5 %) can be commercialized.

14. Preparation of Guava Nectar

Firm ripe fruits of four guava varieties were selected for the preparation of guava nectar. The fruits were washed, sliced blended with equal amount of warm water in a waring blender and sieved to obtain a fine fruit pulp free from seeds and

epicarp. For nectar preparation, 20 % pulp was used. The total soluble solids of pulp were adjusted to 15, 16, 17, 18, 19 and 20o Brix with the addition of calculated amount of sugar and the acidity at 0.3 % in the final product by the addition of required amount of citric acid. The nectar was filtered and the filtrate was filled in to hot sterilized crown bottles of 250 ml capacity with air tight corking. The bottles were pasteurized in boiling water till the temperature of product reached 1000 and stored at ambient condition for 150 days. TSS was determined by hand refractometer. Data revealed that among four varieties of guava, the fruits of Lucknow-49 had maximum TSS, total sugar, reducing and non-reducing sugars as well as ascorbic acid (366.50 mg/100 g). However, the acidity was found medium (0.76 %) having slightly acidic pH (5.51). The data pertaining to biochemical changes in guava nectar prepared from the recipe with 20 % pulp, 170 Brix (TSS) and 0.3 % acidity during storage of five months. The organoleptic score of guava nectar of all the varieties decreased during storage. The nectar prepared from variety L-49 had a higher score followed by Allahabad Safeda, Apple Colour and R-72 in fresh samples and the products of L-49 and Allahabad Safeda were found to be acceptable upto five months of storage. Loss of volatile aromatic substances responsible for flavour and taste of nectar might have decreased organoleptic score as well as acceptability of nectar during storage at ambient condition. (Choudhary *et al.*, 2008).

15. Development & Storage stability of Papaya (*Carica papaya*) Toffee & Leather

This experiment was conducted by Surekha *et al.* (2014) at Dr. Y. S. Parmar University of Horticulture and Forestry, Nauni, Solan. This study efforts were made to develop nutritious and palatable papaya based toffee and leather and to analyze their storage stability at ambient temperature. Sensory quality attribute measured on 9-pointhedonic scale for papaya toffee with best treatment T2 papaya and apricot fruit pulp (50:50) show that color, flavor, taste, texture and overall acceptability rating was higher (8.95, 9.00, 7.5, 7.72, 8.0 respectively) in this treatment at 0 day and negligible changes in its color, flavour, taste, texture and overall acceptability during storage. Henceforth papaya fruits can be blended with acidic fruits to produce a best quality toffee because this fruit is not acidic (0.037 to 0.064 %). This blend for toffee was at par with toffee prepared with papaya and plum (50:50).

16. Evaluation of Fruit Leather made from Two cultivars of Papaya

This experiment was conducted by Zuhair and co-workers in the year 2013 at University Kebangsaan, Malaysia. The objective of this study was to formulate papaya leather from locally grown papaya using natural ingredients like pectin, honey and citric acid. Papaya (*Carica papaya* L. cv. Hongkong and Eksotika) fruits at the mature stage of ripening were collected from Pusat Flora Cheras, Jabatan

Pertanian, and Hulu Langat Semenyih in Selangor, Malaysia. The fruits were selected to ensure uniformity in size (800 g to 1000 g) and color as well as to ensure freedom from diseases and infection.

17. Procedure for making Papaya Fruit Leather

For each cultivar, frozen papaya cultivars were thawed at 40 °C overnight in the fridge. Six hundred grams of thawed papaya cultivars were weighed. Honey 10 % (v/v), 2 % (v/v) of citric acid and 6 % (v/v) of pectin were weighed and mixed with papaya fruits. A Cascade blender model CE071BR (Japan) was used to mix all these ingredients for 2 minutes to make a puree. Cooking oil was lightly sprayed over trays made of stainless steel before 200 g of puree was spread uniformly over the trays with a metal spreader. The drying of the leather was done in the middle section of the cabinet dryer, which had been preheated to 60 ± 2 °C. Throughout the drying interval, the dryness of the leather was closely monitored. Two batches were made for every cultivar each of them has three trays. The trays were dried for 12 hours for both papaya. However, according to the results of the sensory evaluation, panelists expressed a low preference for the Eksotika fruit leather, which received a'moderately liked' score. The results of the present study have great significance for producers of papaya leathers. Among the main factors that determined the acceptability of the fruit leathers were colour, sweetness, sourness, texture and flavour. The end-product can be considered natural, as only small amounts of honey, citric acid and pectin were added in this study. Hence, the consumer requirements for healthy and safe food products were respected.

18. Development of Papaya peel flour based Cookies and evaluation of its quality

This experiment was conducted by Kanta Bokaria and Subhajit Rayin the year 2017 at Guru Nanak Institute of Technology, Kolkata, West Bengal, India. The focus of this research project was to develop papaya peel flour from raw papaya and utilizing the papaya peel flour for the development of Value added cookies. Sensory evaluation revealed that formulated cookies of wheat flour: papaya peel flour (95:5) shows better overall acceptability of 7.6 in comparison to other formulations like wheat flour: papaya peel flour 92.5:7.5 and 90:10 of 6.8 and 6.4 respectively. Moreover, consistent values of other sensory attributes are observed in the former formulations. It is interestingly recorded that though the overall acceptability of the control i.e. wheat flour: papaya peel flour (100:0) is higher i.e.8.0 than 95:5 formulation but due to significant antioxidant and dietary fiber content

19. Development of Jackfruit seed flour incorporated Jackfruit Halwa (*Artocarpus heterophyllus* Lam)

This experiment was conducted by Satheeshan and co-workers in the year 2019 at Kerala Agricultural University, Kerala.

Preparation of Jack fruit halwa

Ingredients used: Jackfruit pulp, Jaggery, Honey, Jack seed flour, Virgin coconut oil, coconut milk, Cashew Nuts, Coconut pieces, Cardamom powder.

Preparation method: Deseeded bulbs extracted from jackfruit weighing 1 kg is steamed and blanched in a cooker for about 10 min till it becomes soft. Blanched bulbs are made into the form of a pulp and homogenized using a blender. Thick coconut milk (500 ml) is added to Jaggery (750 g) and made into the form of syrup by boiling and straining. Virgin coconut oil (120 ml) is added to a pan and heated. When oil is hot, blanched pulp and jaggery/coconut milk syrup added to it. The contents (pulp and syrup) were fried in virgin coconut oil with constant stirring for about one hour till the mixture thickens and become semi solid. Stir continuously and add jack seed flour at various levels, *viz.*, 0 % (control), 5 %, 10 % and 15 % cook for another 30 minutes. At this point, the mixture will attain a semisolid consistency. Add there main ingredients like cardamom powder, fried coconut pieces, cashew nut pieces and stir it continuously till it becomes thick or halwa consistency. Allow the mixture to cool and when it becomes solid, can be cut into shapes, weighed and packed. From the results of the study, it can be concluded that the developed jackfruit halwa is accepted by consumers. It also indicates the immense scope for utilization of jack fruit and seed flour in the preparation of this Value added product by partial replacement of jack pulp in halwa. Based on the results of sensory evaluation, partial replacement of jackfruit pulp with jack seed flour at 10: 90 is selected as the best combination out of all combinations tried. Jackfruit offers exciting possibilities for adding novel products to the food processing industry and contributes towards enhancing the farm income of rural people. Jackfruit and seed have lots of nutrients both macro and micronutrients and other healthy ingredients like virgin coconut oil, coconut milk will add to its nutritive value, taste and flavor to the prepared halwa. It also offers the possibility of diversifying the Value added products in jack fruit and preserve it during off seasons and reducing post-harvest losses.

20. Nutrient analysis of Tender Jackfruit (*Artocarpus heterophyllus*) flour and its incorporation in Breakfast recipes for Diabetics

This experiment was conducted by Christy Paul and Betty Rani Isaac in the year 2017 at St. Teresa's College, Kerala, India.

Processing of the Tender Jackfruit into flour

Food processing is set of methods and techniques used to transform raw ingredients into food or to transform food into other forms for consumption either in home or by the food processing industry. To increase the shelf life and to make it ideal for incorporation into recipes, tender jackfruit can be converted into flour. The processing technique followed by Ex-Service Men's Society, Vettilapara is given below

- Removed the spiny region of tender jackfruit.
- Sliced the remaining tender jackfruit in 1cmthickness uniform size.
- Soaked it in warm water for 10 minutes.
- Tender jackfruit is then kept for freezing at 18 °C for 10 hours.
- Placed the jackfruit outside for cooling processes.
- Set temperature in the dryer at 50 °C and then dried the jackfruit for 8 hours.
- Dried and powdered for product development.

Tender jackfruit flour was incorporated into a total of eight recipes most frequently used by the selected 60 diabetic subjects. Chapati had the highest mean score (4.9) and upma had the lowest mean score (3.8). Rice appam had moderate acceptability. Out of eight breakfast recipes developed, Appam prepared with tender jackfruit flour was not well accepted as it was sticky in consistency. This study revealed that the tender jackfruit flour is rich in fiber and potassium but low in fat. From the survey, conducted to identify the types of breakfast frequently consumed by diabetic patients in Ernakulum, a total of eight recipes such as Chapati, Wheat Dosa, Puttu, Idli, Idiyappam, Appam, Porridge and Upma were selected. Tender jackfruit flour could completely substitute main ingredients in Chapati, Puttu and Idiyappam. As tender jackfruit flour contains 10gm fiber per 100gm recipes prepared with it may have low glycemic index.

21. Quality analysis of Jackfruit Wine

The bulbs were removed and seeds were extracted. Well ripened bulbs were cut into small cubes and all the spices (Cinnamon - 2 inch bark; Poppy seeds - 10 in number; Cardamom- 2 to 3 in number; Star anise - 1 in number; Cloves – 2 to 3 in number) were wrapped in a muslin cloth and kept aside. Water was boiled and

cooled in a vessel with lid. Jack pieces, sugar, and the wrapped spices were added to the boiled water and finally yeast was added for fermentation. The lid was closed tightly and stirred regularly for 30 days. After 30 days, the wine was strained and stored in a clean glass bottle. In wine, T4 (35 % of sugar) was evaluated as the best treatment when compared to others with an alcohol content of 15.72 %, ascorbic acid content of 1.58 mg/100 g, total sugar of 4.08 mg/100 g and TSS of 1.70° Brix. T4 was observed as a sample with maximum shelf life period of more than eight months. The average sensory scores for taste, colour, flavour and overall acceptability of jackfruit wine was initially maximum (colour- 8.5, taste - 7.7, flavour - 8.1 and overall acceptability - 8.1) in T1 with 50 % of sugar concentration followed by T4 (colour - 7.5, taste - 8.0, flavour - 7.7 and overall acceptability - 8.1) during 1st month of evaluation. The same trend was maintained in all months of evaluation with gradual reduction in scores. Cost of production of 1litre of wine was also estimated with a net profit of Rs.132.77 and the benefit cost ratio of 1.74. (Uma Maheswari and Vidhu Valsan, 2019).

22. Conclusion

Fruits having nutritional and health promoting values, so fruit crops are right material for value addition because they are more profitable, has high degree of process ability and richness in health promoting compounds and higher potential for export.

23. Reference

1) Achintya Mahato, Ivi Chakraborty and Bijay Kumar Baidya, 2019. Preparation and evaluation of fruit candy from unripe mango. *International Journal of Chemical Studies.* 8(1): 2727-2731.

2) Aruna .R, Vinaypromodkumar, K. and Sowjanya, K, 2017. Utilization of banana in the development of nutrient rich banana bar. *International Journal of Agricultural Science and Research*: 7(5): 189-194.

3) Christy Paul and Betty Rani Isaac, 2017. Nutrient Analysis of Tender Jackfruit (*Artocarpus heterophyllus*) flour and its incorporation in Breakfast Recipes for Diabetics. *Indian Journal of Research in Food Science and Nutrition,* 4(2): 42-46.

4) Gumte S.V., Tau,r A.T., Sawate, A.R. and Kshirsagar, R.B., 2018. Effect of fortification of mango (*Mangifera indica*) kernel flour on nutritional, phytochemical and textural properties of biscuits. *Journal of Pharmacognosy and Phytochemistry,* 7(3): 1630-1637.

5) Gurumeenakshi, G. and Rajeswari, R. 2020. Development of intermediate moisture sapota slices by osmotic dehydration. *Journal of Pharmacognosy and Phytochemistry,* 9(5): 696 - 699.

6) Haque, E.U., Hanif, M.S., Nadeem, M., Mehmood, A., Ibrar, M., Iqbal, Z., Jabbar, S. Physicochemical and rheological study of orange pulp fortified cookies. *Science Letters*, 3(2): 64 - 67.

7) Hiremath, J. B and Rokhade, A. K. 2012. Preparation and preservation of sapota juice. *International Journal of Food, Agriculture and Veterinary Sciences*, 2(1): 87 - 91.

8) Kanta Bokaria and Subhajit Ray. 2016. Development of Papaya Peel flour based Cookies and evaluation of its quality. *Journal of Multidisciplinary Engineering Science and Technology*, 3(12): 2458 - 9403

9) Laxmi Deepak Bhatlu, M., Ashok Kumar Yadav and Satya Vir Singh. 2014. Preparation of Candy from Kinnow (Citrus) Peel. Global Sustainability Transitions: Impacts and Innovations.

10) Madan Lal Choudhary, S. N. Dikshit Neeraj Shukla and R. R. Saxena. 2008. Evaluation of guava (*Psidium guajava* L.) varieties and standardization of recipe for nectar preparation. *Journal of Horticultural Science*, 3(2): 161 - 163.

11) Minali Masih and Tushar Desale, 2019. Preparation of banana bread to utilize the over ripe banana. *International Journal of Food Science and Nutrition*, 4: 30 -33.

12) Mukta Sinha, Arghya Mani and Prachi Sinha, 2017. Value addition of guava cheese cv. Allahabad safeda by medicinal herbs. *Journal of Pharmacognosy and Phytochemistry*, 6(6): 856-859.

13) Satheeshan K.N., 2019. Development of Jackfruit Seed Flour Incorporated Jackfruit Halwa (*Artocarpus Heterophyllus* Lam). *International Journal of Agriculture Sciences*, 11(22): 9212 - 9215.

14) Surekha Attri, Anju K Dhiman, Manisha Kaushal and Rakesh Sharma. 2014. Development and storage stability of papaya (*Carica papaya* L) toffee and leather. *International Journal of Farm Sciences*, 4(3): 117 - 125.

15) Uma Maheswari, T and Vidhu Valsan. 2019. Quality analysis of jackfruit wine. *International Journal of Life Sciences Research*, 7(1): 98 - 100.

16) Venkata Subbaiah, K., S.L. Jagadeesh, R. Manjula, G. Shali Raju, E. Karunasree, T. Vijaya Nirmala, A. Devivaraprasad Reddy, V. Deepthi, N. Srividya Rani and Reddy, R.V.S.K. 2018. Value Added Studies in Banana as a Commercial Enterprise. *International Journal of Current Microbiology and Applied Science*, 7(3): 3020 - 3024.

17) Zuhair Radhi Addai, Aminah Abdullah, Sahilah Abd. Mutalib and Khalid Hamid Musa. 2016. Evaluation of fruit leather made from two cultivars of papaya. *Italian Journal of Food Science*, 10(7): 28 - 30.

Scientific Advancements in Current Agricultural Research
ISBN: 978-81-947154-7-4
First Edition; 2020
Chapter – 11, Page: 111 - 117

11

FERTIGATION IN VEGETABLE CROPS

R. Rajeswari[*1], P. B. Shabitha[1], Arumugam Shakila[1] and P. Anandan[2]

[1]Department of Horticulture, Faculty of Agriculture, Annamalai University, Annamalai Nagar, Tamil Nadu, India.
[2]Department of Agronomy, Faculty of Agriculture, Annamalai University, Annamalai Nagar, Tamil Nadu, India.

*Corresponding author: rajihorti@gmail.com

Abstract

In modern Agriculture systems, fertigation system is widely practiced as a cost effective and convenient method for applying water soluble fertilizers to crops. Fertilizers can be applied through the system with the irrigation water directly to the region where most of the plants roots develop. Fertigation remarkably improves fertilizer and water use efficiency and with higher yield and quality of agriculture and horticulture crops. Fertilizers for fertigation are selected based on the solubility and compatibility of fertilizers in fertigation system, scheduling fertigation according to crop need, system requirement. Fertigation can be used to avoid problems such as volatilization losses, slow dissolution, and slow fertilizer activation that arises from applying fertilizer onto dryer surface. Furthermore, there is good potential for adoption of drip system in fertigation technique for achieving better productivity and quality in vegetable crops.

Key Words: Fertigation, Cost effective, Water soluble fertilizers and Water use efficiency

1. Introduction

Indian soils are reported as deficient in nutrients, in order to achieve high crop production it is required to supplement nutrients by adding chemical fertilizers and nutrients. These fertilizers are expensive and large quantities of fertilizers are imported to meet the growing demand. On the other hand, Country is facing low fertilizer utilization efficiency; hence there is a need for using fertigation system. Application of fertilizer through irrigation systems is referred as fertigation. The fertilizers are dissolved at appropriate concentrations in water and applied through irrigation water by micro irrigation systems. The nutrients and water in required quantity at correct time are placed in the root zone so that maximum absorption of applied nutrients and water is assured to achieve more crop per drop of water. Fertigation is done with the aid of special fertilizer apparatus called as injectors. There are two types of fertigation viz., Quantitative fertigation and Proportional fertigation and the type of fertigation chosen depends on the crop grown, the soil type and farm management system.

2. Proportional Fertigation

The nutrients are applied in a constant and proportional ratio to the water sheet, so that the irrigation water takes a fixed concentration of the applied fertilizer. In this case the fertilizers are applied by direct injection through fertilizer pumps.

3. Quantitative Fertigation

It is the application of the plant nutrients in predetermined concentrations to the irrigation system. The fertilizer is applied in a pulse after a certain water sheet without fertilizer using a fertilizer tank.

4. Savings in fertilizer and increase in crop yield under fertigation as compared to conventional method of fertilizer application in vegetable crops

Crop	Fertilizer Saving %	Increase in yield %
Tomato	40	33
Okra	40	18
Potato	40	30
Onion	40	16
Broccoli	40	10

5. Objectives of Fertigation

- To maximize yield by optimizing water and fertilizer.
- To use efficiency with reduction in quantity of fertilizer, water and labour.
- To minimize pollution (Yosef, 1997).

6. Key factors to be considered:

- A large range of fertilizer products are suitable for fertigation depending on their physico chemical properties.
- Plant type and stage of growth.
- Soil conditions.
- Water quality.
- Fertilizer availability and price

7. Advantages of Fertigation:

- Increased in yield by 25 - 30 %.
- Improve Fertilizer use efficiency.
- Fertilizer application is more accurate and uniform distribution.
- Nutrients can be applied as per plant requirement.
- Minimizes nutrient losses through leaching & Evaporation.
- Nutrients are immediately available to plant.
- Saving in time, labour, energy.
- Helps in effective weed management.

8. Characteristics of fertilizer suitable for Fertigation:

- High nutrient content, readily available to plants.
- Fully water soluble at field temperature condition.
- No clogging of filters and emitters.
- Low content of insoluble's (less than 0.02 %).
- Compatible with other fertilizers.
- Minimal interaction with irrigation water.
- No drastic changes of water pH.

9. Tamil Nadu government is providing subsidy cost to the farmers

- Drip and fertigation subsidy cost per acre Rs. 32,000.
- Water soluble fertilizer (WSF) subsidy cost per acre Rs. 6000.

In India, micro-irrigation subsidy is covered under the Pradhan Mantri Krishi Sinchayee Yojna (known as PMKSY), which was launched on 1st of July 2015.

10. Response of vegetable crops to fertigation:

In tomato, Badr and Abou (2007) conducted an experiment on the effect of fertigation frequency from subsurface drip irrigation on yield of crop grown on sandy soil and the results of the study revealed that the highest total fruit yield was recorded with the fertigation frequencies of 1, 3 and 7 days respectively. Shaymaa *et al.* (2009) conducted an experiment on the effect of method and rate of fertilizer application under drip irrigation on yield and nutrient uptake and the results revealed that fertigation at 100% NPK water soluble fertilizers significantly increased the yield. Singh *et al.,* (2013) conducted an experiment on the effect of various fertigation schedules, organic manures, yield and fertilizer use efficiency under arid condition and concluded that application of compost 5t ha^{-1} + 2 t ha^{-1} lignite, daily method of fertigation and 100 % recommended dose of NPK fertilizer resulted better as compare to other treatments in tomato.

In rabi onion, Prabhakar *et al.* (2011) conducted an experiment on the effect of microsprinkler fertigation on growth and yield and the results indicated that the fertigation treatments were superior for marketable bulb yield as compared to soil application of fertilizer.

In sweet pepper, Pandey *et al.* (2013) conducted an experiment on the effect of drip irrigation, spacing and nitrogen fertigation on productivity and the results revealed that the maximum yield, minimal disease and saved water and total irrigation time as compared to top dressing.

Prabhakar *et al.* (2013) conducted an experiment on the influence of various sources and levels of fertilizer applied through fertigation and it is evident that application of 70 or 100% recommended NPK, through fertigation using water-soluble fertilizers resulted in higher yield in hybrid watermelon.

In cucumber, Patil and Gadge (2016) concluded that the application of 125 per cent NPK through drip irrigation recorded maximum yield and also showed maximum net income followed by application of 125 per cent N through drip irrigation and soil application of P and K as basal dose.

Chand *et al.* (2017) conducted an experiment on the effect of fertigation and bio-fertilizers on growth and yield attributes and the results shown that application of fertigation levels (F75) significantly increased yield attributes in sprouting broccoli.

Nair *et al.* (2017) conducted an experiment on the growth and yield performance in relation to fertigation using different rates and sources of fertilizers and the results revealed that the application of recommended dose using water soluble fertilizers through 100 per cent weekly fertigation resulted in highest marketable yield in okra.

In bitter gourd, Abraham *et al.* (2018) conducted an experiment on the effect of drip irrigation, fertigation and mulching on growth and dry matter accumulation and the results indicated that the irrigation and fertigation levels along with plastic mulching significantly enhanced the length of main vine, number of primary branches, dry matter content of leaves and vine, fruit dry mater content, harvest index and N, P, K and iron content of fruits.

Nayak *et al.* (2018) conducted an experiment on the effect of fertigation and mulching on growth, yield and yield attributing characteristics and the results revealed that the maximum values for the yield attributing traits such as length of fruit, single fruit weight, minimum number of days taken for 50 % flowering and post- harvest parameters such as duration of maximum retention of shelf life, percentage of marketable fruits was recorded with the application of 100 percent N, P and K (RDF) through fertigation and mulching which remained at par with treatment where 80 percent N, P and K is applied through fertigation and mulching in pointed gourd

Hayyawi and Qusay (2019) concluded that good productivity was achieved through adoption of fertigation combined with Nano N, P, K fertilizers and good irrigation management with drip irrigation, high water use efficiency as well as a consistent distribution of nutrients in the soil in potato.

In brinjal, Hadole *et al.* (2020) revealed that plant height, number of branches per plant, number of leaves, number of fruits per plant, average weight of fruit, yield of fruits per plant, leaf dry matter, fruit dry matter and total dry matter was improved with increased fertigation level as compared to traditional application of fertilizers.

In ridge gourd, Ananda Murthy *et al.* (2020) concluded that fertigation with water soluble fertilizers of 150:90:150 kg NPK ha^{-1} is best for getting better growth, yield and nutrient uptake and also for buildup of plant available nutrients in the soil.

In cabbage, Nikzad *et al.* (2020) revealed that application of 100 % RDF in 12 equal splits at 5 days intervals significantly recorded maximum plant height and plant spread in East-West and North-South directions at 45 and 60 days after transplanting and at harvest respectively. The same treatment recorded highest

Chapter - 11

individual head weight, head length, head diameter, head volume, head width, yield per plot and yield per hectare.

11. Conclusion

It is concluded that fertigation can play significant role in application of accurate daily dosage of nutrients at clearly fixed times, with planned cycles, thus maximizing yields, reducing costs both of manpower and of equipment, protecting crops from contamination. Fertigation can play significant role in vegetable cultivation not only to increase the yield and it increase the quality of vegetables, but also increase water use efficiency and nutrient use efficiency. This requires creating better awareness and education both for extension workers and farmers. In other words, we can say that the fertigation technology is now the need of the hour.

12. References

1) Abraham, R. K., M. Partha Sarathi and D. Chandra Manna. 2018. Effect of drip irrigation, fertigation and mulching on growth and dry matter accumulation in bitter gourd. *Journal of Krishi Vigyan*, 6(2): 61 - 67.

2) Ananda Murthy, H. C., A. K. Nair, D. Kalaivanan, M. Anjanappa, S. Shankara Hebbar and R. H. Laxman. 2020. Effect of NPK fertigation on post-harvest soil nutrient status, nutrient uptake and yield of hybrid ridge gourd (*Luffa acutangula* (L.) Roxb) Arka Vikram. *International Journal of Chemical Studies*, 8(4): 3064 -3069.

3) Badr, M. A and A. A. Abou El-Yazied. 2007. Effect of fertigation frequency from subsurface drip irrigation on tomato yield grown on sandy soil. *Australian Journal of Basic and Applied Sciences*, 1(3): 279 - 285.

4) Chand, P., S. Mukherjee and Vivek Kumar. 2017. Effect of Fertigation and Biofertilizers on growth and yield attributes of Sprouting Broccoli (*Brassica oleracea* var. *italica*) Cultivar Fiesta. *International Journal of Pure and Applied Biological Sciences*, 5(4): 144 - 149.

5) Hadole, S. S., Gopal Patidar, P. A Sarap, A. B Age, E. Sathyanarayan and J. N. Parmar. 2020. Effect of fertigation on growth, quality and yield of Brinjal. *Journal of Pharmacogenetics and Phytochemistry*, 9(3): 526 - 530.

6) Hayyawi W. A. Al-Juthery and Qusay M. N. Al-Shami. 2019. The Effect of Fertigation with Nano NPK Fertilizers on some parameters of growth and yield of potato (*Solanum tuberosum* L.). *Al-Qadisiyah Journal of Agricultural Sciences*, 9(2): 225 - 232.

7) Nair, A. K., S. S. Hebbar, M. Prabhakar and R. S. Rajeshwari. 2017. Growth and yield performance of Okra (*Abelmoschus esculentus* (L.) Moench. in relation to Fertigation using different rates and sources of Fertilizers. *International Journal of Current Microbiology and Applied Sciences*, 6(8): 137 - 143.

8) Nayak, H., D. Sahoo, S. C. Swain, B. Jena, P. Pradhan and D. Paramjita. 2018. Effect of fertigation and mulching on growth, yield and yield attributing characteristics of pointed gourd (*Trichosanthes dioica* Roxb.) CV. Swarna Alaukik. *International Journal of Chemical Studies*, 6(2): 258 - 261.

9) Nikzad, M., J. S. Aravinda Kumar, M. Anjanappa, H. Amarananjundeswara, B. N. Dhananjaya and G. Basavaraj. 2020. Effect of Fertigation levels on growth and yield of Cabbage (*Brassica oleracea* L. var. *capitata*). *International Journal of Current Microbiology and Applied Sciences*, 9(1): 1240 - 1247.

10) Pandey, A. K., A. K. Singh, A. Kumar and S. K. Singh. 2013. Effect of Drip Irrigation, Spacing and Nitrogen Fertigation on Productivity of Chilli (*Capsicum annuum* L.). *Environment and Ecology*, 31(1): 139 - 142.

11) Patil, M and S. B. Gadge. 2016. Yield response of cucumber (*Cucumis sativus* L.) to different fertigation levels. *International Journal of Agricultural Engineering*, 9(2): 145 - 149.

12) Prabhakar, M., S. S. Hebbar and A. K. Nair. 2011. Effect of microsprinkler fertigation on growth and yield of Rabi onion. *Journal of Horticultural Science*, 6(1): 66 - 68.

13) Prabhakar, M., S. S. Hebbar and A. K. Nair. 2013. Influence of various sources and levels of fertilizer applied through fertigation on hybrid watermelon grown in rabi summer. *Journal of Horticultural Science*, 8(1): 60 - 64

14) Shaymaa I. Shedeed, Sahar M. Zaghloul and A. A. Yassen. 2009. Effect of Method and rate of Fertilizer application under Drip Irrigation on yield and nutrient uptake by Tomato. *Ozean Journal Applied Science*, 2(2): 236 - 239.

15) Singh, A., I. J. Gulati and Rahul Chopra. (2013). Effect of various fertigation schedules and organic manures on tomato (*Lycopersicon esculentum* mill.) yield under arid condition. *International Quarterly Journal of Life Science*, 8(4): 1261 -1264.

Scientific Advancements in Current Agricultural Research
ISBN: 978-81-947154-7-4
First Edition; 2020
Chapter – 12, Page: 118 - 125

12

POTENTIALITIES OF ENHANCING ANTIOXIDANTS IN VEGETABLE CROPS

P. Madhanakumari and M. Mahalakshmi

Department of Horticulture, Faculty of Agriculture, Annamalai University, Annamalai Nagar, Tamil Nadu, India

Abstract

Malnutrition is one of the major problems of humans globally, especially in resource poor developing countries distressing the economic, social and personal growth. Vegetables are an indispensable source of powerful antioxidants which represent multiple properties beneficial for human health. Vegetables have thus had conferred as the 'functional foods. Improving the antioxidant in the plant parts has become the goal for vegetable breeding because of increasing awareness towards human nutrition and health. A large diversity in antioxidant content has been found among cultivars and wild relatives. Identification of sources of variation of antioxidants content can be accomplished by screening of germplasm collection, also through morphological characters and origin. Modern genomics and biotechnological strategies such as CRISPR, Agrobacterium mediated transformation are powerful tools for identification of genomic region and genes with a key role in accumulation of antioxidants in vegetables. We anticipate that the combination of conventional and modern strategies will facilitate the development of a new generation of vegetable varieties with enhanced content in antioxidants.

Key words: Antioxidants, *Agrobacterium*, CRISPR, RNAi, Polyphenol and Lycopene

1. Introduction

Life on earth as we know it, began with complete awareness of the surroundings. In other words, a constant, undying interaction between matter and energy engendered what we call life. Nutritional deficiency is one of the major problems globally, especially in resource poor developing countries distressing the economic, social and personal growth simultaneously. Vegetables are an indispensable component of balanced diets as they provide different vitamins, minerals, dietary fiber and phytonutrients required for growth and development of human beings; and are the best and cheapest sources of nutrients particularly to the vegetarians. Presently, improving the nutrient concentration in edible plant parts has become a goal of plant/vegetable breeding because of the increasing public awareness towards human nutrition and health (Karmakar *et al.*, 2016). The use of biotechnological tool and molecular marker assisted selection will certainly expedite the pace and prospects of success for "nutrient biofortification" of vegetable crops.

To deal with the free radicals or so-called ROS, the human body is equipped with an effective defence system which includes various enzymes and high and low molecular weight antioxidants. Antioxidants neutralize free radicals by donating one of their own electrons, ending the electron-stealing reaction. The antioxidants do not themselves become free radicals by donating electrons because they are stable in their form. These act as scavengers and play the housekeeper's role by mopping up free radicals before they get a chance to create havoc in a body. Thus, they may well be defined as the substances that are capable of quenching or stabilizing free radicals (Kaur et al., 2001).

2. Classification of Antioxidants

Based on their Activity

a) *Enzymatic*: Breaking down and removing free radicals.
b) *Non-enzymatic*: Interrupting free radical chain reactions. Natural and Synthetic.

Based on their Solubility

a) *Water soluble:* Vitamin C, Glutathione, Urate, Bilirubin.
b) *Lipid soluble:* Vitamin E, Lycopene, Lutein, Zeaxanthin.

Based on their Defense mechanism

a) *Preventive:* Vitamin-E, Ascorbic acid, Beta-carotene
b) *Interceptive:* Glutathione, Superoxide dismutase.

Based on their Size

a) *Small-molecule antioxidants:* Vitamin C, E, Carotenoids and Glutathione.

b) *Large-molecule antioxidants:* Super Oxide Dismutase and catalase

Based on their Origins

a) *Endogenous Antioxidants*: Bilirubin, Glutathione, Ubiquinone (coenzyme Q10) and Uric acid.

b) *Dietary Antioxidants:* Vitamin C, Vitamin E, Betacarotene and Polyphenols.

3. Methods to enhance Antioxidants

a) Conventional Breeding

Conventional breeding techniques, based on selection and hybridization, have shown a high potential for enhancing the content of antioxidants in a wide range of plants. Genetic improvement of antioxidants content can be accomplished by different techniques, like simple mass selection or individual selection of plants with desirable characteristics for seed or vegetative propagation, or through the deliberate crossing of closely or distantly related individuals in order to produce new crop varieties or hybrids with increased contents. Genetic variation is necessary for efficient and successful selection and breeding for increased antioxidant content, usually most of their variation is quantitative rather than qualitative. Therefore, in general the conventional selection and breeding methods to be used for enhancing the antioxidants content in vegetables will be those of quantitative traits.

b) Genetic Engineering – A Novel tool for Nutrition enhancement

During recent times, the requirement in farming has altered towards the importance of crop varieties with improved nutritional and quality traits. During the last three decades, breeding objectives have prioritized for the growing attention for obtaining new standard of quality traits, more particularly nutritive and nutraceutical value (Kumar *et al.*, 2009). Major genetic engineering tools are

(i)   *Agrobacterium* mediated transfer

(ii)   CRISPR/Cas 9 and

(iii)   RNA- interference.

(i) *Agrobacterium* mediated Transformation

Agrobacterium is considered as the nature genetic engineer. *Agrobacterium tumefaciens* is a rod shaped, gram negative bacteria found in the soil that causes tumorous growth termed as crown gall disease in dicot plants. This DNA segment

(transfer DNA or T-DNA) is present on large plasmid called Tumor- inducing (Ti) plasmids in the bacterium. The T-DNA (about 20 kb long) is integrated into the plant chromosome by recombination. A series of virulence (*vir*) genes are involved in directing the infection process. So, when a plant root or a stem is wounded it gives off certain response.

(ii) CRISPR/Cas 9 System

CRISPR-Cas9 (Clustered Regularly Interspaced Short Palindromic Repeats) is a genome editing tool that is creating a buzz in the science world. It is faster, cheaper and more accurate than previous techniques of editing DNA and has a wide range of potential applications. It is currently the simplest, most versatile and precise method of genetic manipulation and is therefore causing a buzz in the science world.

(iii) RNA-interference

RNAi is the most efficient tool for targeted gene silencing. RNAi is now routinely utilized across multiple biological disciplines to determine gene function. RNAi is also being utilized for therapeutic interventions to downregulate the expression of genes involved in disease pathogenesis. The current review is focused on recent advancements in the biology and applications of RNAi.

4. Polyphenols

These are naturally occurring secondary metabolites in plants generally involved in defence mechanism. These are non-nutritive, health promoting, bioactive compounds. More than 8000 polyphenols are reported. It contains one or more phenolic rings.It has protective effect on the DNA damage caused by the hydroxyl radicals.

Kaushik *et al.* (2015) observed the various levels of chlorogenic acidin various vegetables like Artichoke (*Cynara scolymus* L.) 0.4 – 7.3 g/kg, Carrot (*Daucus carota*), 0.3 – 18.8 g/kg, Chicory (*Cichorium intybus* L.), 0.1 – 0.9 g/kg, Eggplant (*Solanum melongena*) 1.4 – 28.0 g/kg, Lettuce (*Lactuca sativa* L.) 0.1 – 0.3 g/kg and Pepper (*Capsicum annuum*) 0.7 – 0.9 g/kg.

Tomato (*Solanum esculentum*) 0.2 – 0.4 g/kg. The variation, which can be of several fold differences among accessions of the same species, can be exploited to select varieties with higher content in phenolic acids or to identify parental materials for breeding programmes.

Somavathi *et al.* (2014) observed that there was a significant difference between the skin colour/pattern and antioxidant activity. Total phenolic content (TPC) and FRAP values of brinjal extracts varied from 48.67±0.27 to 61.11±0.26 mg GAE/100 g fresh weight and 4.19±0.11 to 7.46±0.26 mmol of $FeSO_4$/g fresh weight, respectively. Brinjal with dark purple lines (S3) showed the highest antioxidant activity as quantified by FRAP and TPC while brinjal with light purple lines (S2) showed the least. Purple brinjal with no lines (S1) displayed the highest DPPH radical scavenging activity with an IC50 value of 3.51±0.62 mg/ml while S3 demonstrated the strongest total antioxidant activity as measured by ABTS assay with an inhibition of 40.45 %. In the FTC assay, the percent inhibition of linoleic acid oxidation ranged from 15.11±1.31 to 26.74±2.85.

In an attempt to manipulate pigment biosynthesis to increase the health benefits of vegetables, the effect of the maize *Lc* regulatory locus on flavonoid content was assessed in a *Brassica oleracea* line. Transgenic plants showed increased anthocyanin content on transfer to high light conditions. In addition, plants showed increased antioxidant activity. DNA was isolated from leaves of in vitro shoots and analysed by PCR for the NPTII gene using the method and primers described in Christey *et al.* (2011) to produce a 600 bp fragment. A fragment of the expected size (486 bp) was obtained in all lines. PCR analysis has confirmed the presence of both genes in over 20 independent transgenic plants.

5. Lycopene

Li *et al.* (2018) studied that the pYL CRISPR/Cas9 multi-target editing system was successfully applied to create mutations of many related genes in carotenoid synthesis and metabolic pathways in tomato plants by artificially introducing a transformation vector containing multiple sgRNA expression cassettes to increase the content of lycopene in fruit. This study provides the basis for acquiring new tomato varieties with improved agricultural traits.

6. Vitamin C

Clifford (2000) found differences in the expression pattern and gene structure of the two members of the *GME* family in tomato plants. The constitutive expression of *SlGME1* or *SlGME2* gene resulted in increased AsA content in tomato leaves and fruits, improving tolerance to several abiotic stresses. Further experimental efforts are necessary to verify whether the simultaneous overproduction of *SlGME1* and *SlGME2* by crossing these two transgenic lines would result in a greater increase in tomato AsA.

7. ß carotene

It serves as precursors for the biosynthesis of the plant hormone abscisic acid and for the production of volatile compounds for fruit and flower flavour and aroma (Bouvier *et al.*, 2003; Simkin *et al.*, 2004).

Lu *et al.* (2006) revealed that, or as a novel regulatory gene functions across different plant species to enhance carotenoid accumulation. Manipulating the formation of chromoplasts for carotenoid accumulation, together with increased expression of the catalytic components of the carotenoid biosynthetic pathway, may prove to be a more effective strategy for enhancing carotenoid levels in food crops to the levels required for optimal human nutrition and health.

8. Constraints for Transgenic Vegetable Breeding

Generally, there are many cultivars of the same vegetable species on the market and the life span of an individual cultivar can be quite short. Introducing a transgene into a breeding program can be complicated and cost prohibitive, especially in crops with difficulty for using backcrossing (e.g cassava, potato or sweet potato). Because of the regulatory costs currently involved with GM vegetable crops, it is difficult for either the public or private sector to develop novel products specifically for small vegetable markets, including specialty vegetable crops in the developed and developing world and almost any crop in countries with relatively small agricultural sectors.

9. Future Perspectives

The biggest hurdle in the commercial use of GM crops is the regulatory approval process which is very expensive and time consuming. Biofortification is a promising agriculturally based strategy for improving the nutritional status of malnourished populations throughout the world. Therefore, major resources should be allocated to biofortification programs.

10. Safety of Transgenic crops

The World Health Organization, the Food and Agriculture Organization of the United Nations, the Royal Society of London, the US National Academy of Sciences, the Brazilian Academy of Sciences, the Chinese Academy of Sciences, the Indian National Science Academy, the Mexican Academy of Sciences and the Third World Academy of Sciences, the American College of Nutrition, the Society of Toxicology, the British Medical Association and the Union of German Academies of Sciences and Humanities, among others, have stated that GM crops approved for commercialization, do not pose more risk to human health than conventional crops,

and they should be considered as safe as conventional ones. The world has witnessed a steady increase of transgenic crop area in the last 1.5 decades.

11. Conclusion

Biofortification provides a feasible means of reaching malnourished populations in relatively remote rural areas, delivering naturally fortified foods to people with limited access to commercially-marketed fortified foods, which are more readily available in urban areas. Biofortification and commercial fortification, therefore, are highly complementary. Ultimately, good nutrition depends on adequate intakes of a range of nutrients and other compounds, in combinations and levels that are not yet completely understood. Thus, the best and final solution to eliminating under nutrition as a public health problem in developing countries is to provide increased consumption of a range of non-staple foods. However, this will require several decades to be realised, informed government policies, and a relatively large investment in agricultural research and other public and on-farm infrastructure.

12. References

1) Charanjit Kaur, Harish C. Kapoor. 2001. Antioxidants in fruits and vegetables -the millennium's Health. *International Journal of Food Science and Technology*, 36: 703 – 725.

2) Christey, M. C., R. H. Braun, E. L. Conner, J. K. Reader, D. W. R. White and C. R. Voisey. 2006. Agrobacterium-mediated transformation of *Brassica oleracea* with the Lc Locus. *GM Crops.* 3: 327 – 328.

3) Karamkar, P., B. K. Singh, Jyothi Devi, P. M. Singh and B. Singh. 2016. Genetic improvement for improving nutritional quality in vegetable crops: A review. *Vegetable Science*, 43(2): 145 - 155.

4) Kumar, S., R. K. Volz, P. A. Alspach and V. G. M. Bus. 2009. Development of a recurrent apple breeding programme in New Zealand: A synthesis of results, and a proposed revised breeding strategy. *Euphytica.*, doi:10.1007/s10681-0090090-6.

5) Luo, Z., Zhang. J, Li. J, Yang. C, Wang. T and Ouyang. B. 2013. A STAYGREEN protein SlSGR1 regulates lycopene and beta-carotene accumulation by interacting directly with SlPSY1 during ripening processes in tomato. *New Phytology*, 198: 442 - 452.

6) Mayer, J. E., W. H. Pfeiffer and P. Beyer. 2008. Biofortified crops to alleviate micronutrient malnutrition. *Current Opinion in Plant Biology*, 11: 166 - 170.

7) Prashant Kaushik, Isabel Andújar, Santiago Vilanova, Mariola Plazas, Pietro Gramazio, Francisco Javier Herraiz, Navjot Singh Brar and Jaime Prohens. 2015. Breeding Vegetables with Increased Content in Bioactive Phenolic Acids. *Molecules*, 20: 18464 – 18481.

8) Shan Lu, Joyce Van Eck, Xiangjun Zhou, Alex B. Lopez, Diana M. O'Halloran, Kelly M. Cosman, Brian J. Conlin, Dominick J. Paolillo, David F. Garvin, Julia Vrebalov, Leon V. Kochian, Hendrik Kupper, Elizabeth D. Earle, Jun Cao, and Li Lia. The Cauliflower or Gene Encodes a DnaJ Cysteine-Rich Domain-Containing Protein That Mediates High Levels of b-Carotene Accumulation. *The Plant Cell*, 18: 3594 - 3605.

9) Somawathi, K. M., V. Rizliya and D. Wijesinghe. 2014. Antioxidant activity and total phenolic activity of different coloured brinjal. *Tropical Agriculture*, 22: 205 -213.

10) Xindi Li, Yanning Wang, Sha Chen, HuiqinTiaz, Daqi Fu, Benzhong Zhu, Yunbo Luo and Hongliang Zhu. 2018. Lycopene is enriched in Tomato fruit by CRISPR/Cas9-Mediated Multiplex Genome Editing. *Frontiers in Plant Science*, 9: 559.

Scientific Advancements in Current Agricultural Research
ISBN: 978-81-947154-7-4
First Edition; 2020
Chapter – 13, Page: 126 - 143

13

Trichoderma SPP. - A BIOCONTROL AGENT FOR SUSTAINABLEMANAGEMENT OF PLANT DISEASES

J. Jayachitra[1], P. Sivasakthivelan[1], G. Kumaresan[1] and S. Sudhasha[2]

[1]Department of Agricultural Microbiology, Faculty of Agriculture, Annamalai University, Annamalai Nagar – 608 002, Tamil Nadu, India.

[2]Department of Plant Pathology, Faculty of Agriculture, Annamalai University, Annamalai Nagar – 608 002, Tamil Nadu, India.

Abstract

Trichoderma spp. are mainly asexual fungi that are present in all types of agricultural soils and also in decaying wood. The antagonistic activity of *Trichoderma* species showed that it is parasitic on many soil-borne and foliage pathogens. The fungus is also a decomposer of cellulosic waste materials. Recent discoveries show that the fungi not only act as biocontrol agents, but also stimulate plant resistance, and plant growth and development resulting in an increase in crop production. The biocontrol activity involving mycoparasitism, antibiotics and competition for nutrients, also induces defence responses or systemic resistance responses in plants. These responses are an important part of *Trichoderma* in biocontrol program. Currently, *Trichoderma* spp., is being used to control plant diseases in sustainable diseases management systems. This paper reviews the published information on *Trichoderma* spp., and its biocontrol activity in sustainable disease management programs.

Keywords: *Trichoderma,* Biocontrol potential, Antibiotics and Agriculture.

1. Introduction

Fungal species belonging to the genus Trichoderma are worldwide in occurrence and easily isolated from soil, decaying wood, and other forms of plant organic matter. They are, for the most part, classified as imperfect fungi, in that they have no known sexual stage. Rapid growth rate in culture and the production of numerous spores (conidia) that are varying shades of green characterize fungi in this genus. The reverse side of colonies is often uncoloured, buff, yellow, amber, or yellow-green, and many species produce prodigious quantities of thick-walled spores (chlamydospores) in submerged mycelium (Gamsand Bisset, 1998). The potential of *Trichoderma* species as biocontrol agents of plant diseases was first recognized in the early 1930s (Weindling, 1934), and in subsequent years, control of many diseases has been added to the list (Aluko and Hering, 1970; Harman, 2000; Wells *et al.*, 1972; Yedidia *et al.*, 1999). This has culminated in the commercial production of several *Trichoderma* species for the protection and growth enhancement of a number of crops in the United States, and in the production of *Trichoderma* species and mixtures of species in India, Israel, New Zealand, and Sweden (D. R. Fravel, personal communication). One of the most interesting aspects of the science of biological control is the study of the mechanisms employed by biocontrol agents to effect disease control. Past research indicates that the mechanisms are many and varied, even within the genus *Trichoderma*. In order to make the most effective use of biocontrol agents for the control of plant diseases, we must understand how the agents work and what their limitations are. We can then develop effective means of culturing, storing, applying, and utilizing biocontrol agents so that we harness their best effort for disease.

2. *Trichoderma* Biology

Mycoflora belonging to genus *Trichoderma* usually cosmopolitan shows a high level of genetic diversity and frequently found in varying habitats (Grinyer *et al.*, 2004; Samuels, 2006; Zhang *et al.*, 2007). *Trichoderma* species have been easily isolated from natural soil, decaying plant organic matter and wood and is classified as imperfect fungi belonging to order Hypocreales of Ascomycota (Howell, 2003; Küçük and Kivanç, 2003). *Trichoderma* multiplies and grows very fast in different nutrient sources such as Malt Agar (MA), Czapek Dox Agar (CDA) as well as Potato Dextrose Agar (PDA) and produces conidia/spores of various shades characterized by green colour (Chaverri *et al.*, 2003; Rey *et al.*, 2001) and some species produce thick walled chlamydospores (Lu *et al.*, 2004). The salient feature of this genus is the ability to parasitize other pathogenic fungal mycoflora specially associated with root rot and wilt diseases (Santoro *et al.*, 2014). *Trichoderma* species

have been reported as endophytic fungi while generally found in all types of soils such as agricultural soil, orchard soil as well as forest soil as opportunistic plant symbionts (Chaverri *et al.*, 2011) and usually considered successful competitor of plant pathogens (Kim *et al.*, 2012).

3. Morphological characteristics

Morphological based identification of *Trichoderma* species is a primary method of identification that is not a precise method to differentiate diversity between species (Zhang *et al.*, 2005). *Trichoderma* species are fast growing under the optimum range between 25 - 30 °C (Latifian *et al.*, 2007). *Trichoderma* used a variety of compounds such as carbon and nitrogen sources as a growth medium for its sporulation (Gao *et al.*, 2007) and sporulates of *Trichoderma* abundantly produce powder masses characterized by green conidia (Chaudhari *et al.*, 2011) which is diagnostic tool that is also found in related and unrelated genera such as *Myrothecium*, *Clonostachys* and *Aspergillus* as well as *Penicillium* respectively (Alvindia and Hirooka, 2011). Conidiophore is not well defined but mostly branched contains unicellular conidia and phialides at the tip of branched hyphal system that cannot be seen on one week old media (Lu *et al.*, 2004). Generally, conidia shape is ellipsoidal to oblong and some *Trichoderma* species have globose to subglobose with the length/width ratio 1.4 and 1 - 3 respectively (Bissett *et al.*, 2003; Jaklitsch *et al.*, 2006) while few species have smooth conidia (Samuels *et al.*, 2002). Conidia color morphology varies from species to species but typically green or may be gray, white and yellow (Jaklitsch *et al.*, 2006).

4. Importance of *Trichoderma*

The perspective character of *Trichoderma* species as biological control of fungal plant pathogens was first introduced in the early 1930s and later on research indicates that it can control effectively foliar, seed and specially soil-borne pathogenic fungi belong to various genera (El-Mohamedy and Alla, 2013; Gveroska and Ziberoski, 2012). *Trichoderma* species are opportunistic, avirulent, and plant symbionts that can compete as well as survive in the complex ecosystem (Harman *et al.*, 2004b). Although, these are capable of successful root colonizer and their number increases when abundant healthy roots are present in the ecosystem (Brotman *et al.*, 2008) and protect the roots and plants from pathogens as well as diseases (Howell, 2003). They increase plant resistant ability against drought conditions and promote the growth of a plant by phosphate, micro-nutrients, and solubilization (Kumar, 2013). Some species of *Trichoderma* are efficient producer of extracellular enzymes that degrade complex compounds of polysaccharides and also used commercially (Samanta *et al.*, 2012). *Trichoderma* species are environmental friendly (Singh *et al.*,

2008) and an alternative to synthetic chemicals (Gupta and Dikshit, 2010) that developed symbiotic relationship with plants rather than parasitic relationship reduced chances of behavioral changes in human caused by the use of synthetic chemicals (Brimner and Boland, 2003).

5. Plant growth enhancement by *Trichoderma* species

Trichoderma spp. not only controlled pathogens, they also enhance plant growth and root development (biofertilizer) and stimulate plant defense mechanisms (Harman *et al.*, 2004b). Some *Trichoderma* strains have been shown to penetrate the epidermis and establish robust and long-lasting colonization of root surfaces. *Trichoderma* spp. has been shown to improve growth of lettuce, tomato, and pepper plants (Vinale *et al.*, 2008). In a study of maize plants, several months after treatment with *T. harzianum* strain T-22, the plant roots were about twice as long when compared to untreated plants. *Trichoderma* spp. also produced gluconic and citric acids, decreased the soil pH, and enhanced the solubilization of phosphates, micronutrients, and mineral components such as iron, magnesium, and manganese (Vinale *et al.*, 2008).

Table 1: Efficacy of *Trichoderma* species against soil-borne fungal pathogens

Trichoderma strains	Pathogen(s)	Plant/ Crop	Disease	Efficacy (Inhibition)	Experiment
T. harzianum	*Rhizoctonia solani*	Tomato	Wilt	5 %	Pot Exp.
T. viride *T. harzinum*	*Fusarium solani*	Tomato	Root rot	70-72 %	*In vitro*
T. harzianum *T. viride*	*R. solani*	Tomato	Damping off	51 %	*In vitro*
T. viride (Tv-R) *T. harzianum* *T. viride* *T. virens*	*M. phaseolina*	Chick pea	Dry root rot	62 %	Laboratory conditions
T. harzianum *T. viride* *T. virens*	*R. bataticola*	Mung bean	Dry root rot	87 %	Pot and field conditions
T. harzianum	*Botrytis cinerea*				
T. harzianum	*F. oxysporum* f. sp. *Radiciscucumerinum*	Cucumber	Stem and root rot	12-79 %	Pots experiments

6. Plant root colonization by *Trichoderma* spp.

Studies of the early invading fungi *Trichoderma* spp. showed that root colonization stimulated plant defense responses such as induction of peroxidases, chitinases, β-1, 3 glucanase, phenylalanine, and hydroperoxidase lyase; activated signaling of biosynthetic pathways; and caused accumulation of low-molecular weight phytoalexins (Yedidia *et al.*, 2003). Therefore, the interaction appears to be a symbiotic relationship in which *Trichoderma* lives in the nutritional niche provided by the plant, and the plant was protected from disease.

7. Uses of *Trichoderma* spp.

The discovery of cellulase production by *Trichoderma reesei*, which was isolated by Reese (1976), led to it becoming a very important cellulase or enzyme producer.

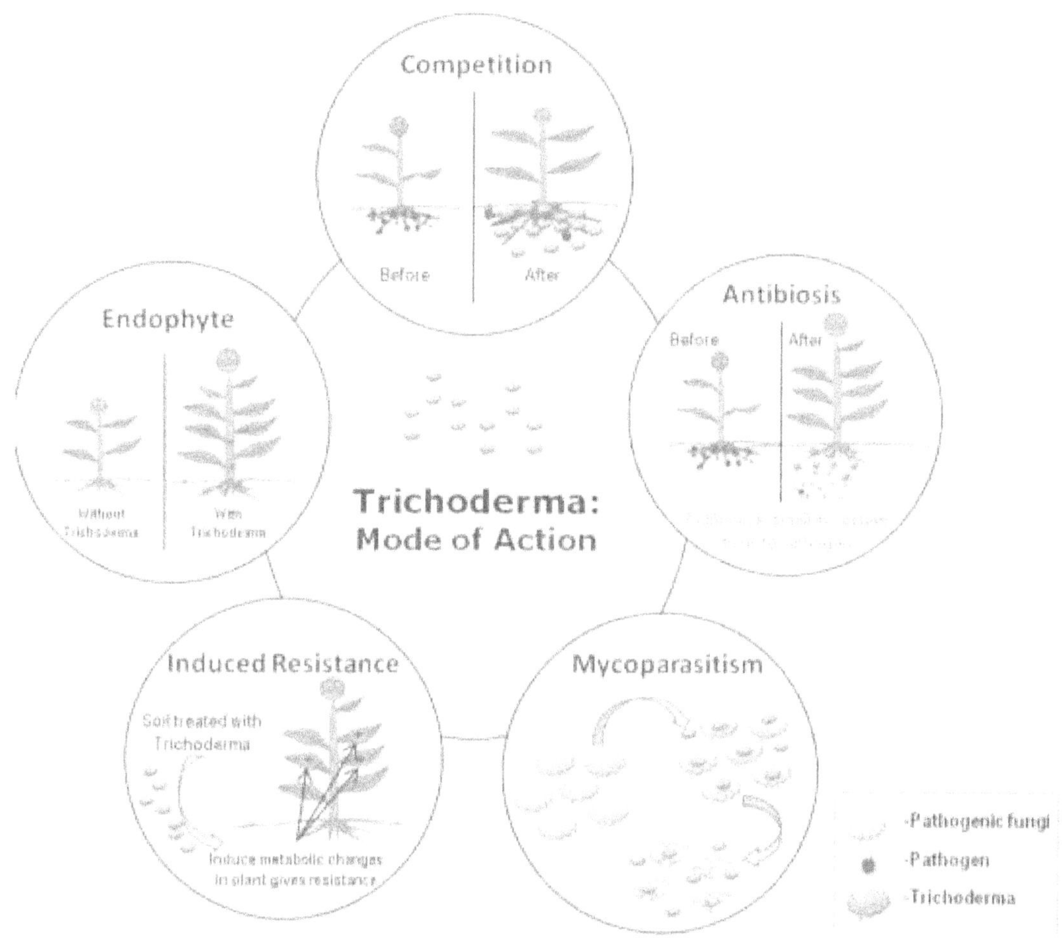

Figure – 1: Model depicting mode of action of *Trichoderma* spp. against pathogen and plant growth improvement

8. Biocontrol by competition for nutrients and living space

Trichoderma spp., are rapidly growing fungi that have persistent conidia and a broad spectrum of substrate utilization. They are very efficient competitors for nutrition and living space (Hjeljord *et al.*, 2000). In addition, *Trichoderma* spp., are naturally resistant to many toxic compounds, including herbicides, fungicides, and phenolic compounds. Therefore, they can grow rapidly and impact pathogens by producing metabolic compounds that impede spore germination (fungistasis), kill the cells (antibiosis), or modify the rhizosphere, (e.g. by acidifying the soil so that the pathogens cannot grow) (Benitez *et al.*, 2004). Starvation is the most common cause of death for microorganisms, so competition for limited nutrients is especially important in the biocontrol of phytopathogens. Iron uptake is essential for filamentous fungi and under iron starvation; fungi excrete low-molecular weight ferriciron-specific chelators, termed siderophores. *Trichoderma* spp. produce highly efficient siderophores that chelate iron and stop the growth of other fungi (Benitez *et al.*, 2004). Therefore, soil characteristics influence *Trichoderma* as a biocontrol agent.

9. Biocontrol by Mycoparasitism

The direct interaction between *Trichoderma* and pathogen is called Mycoparasitism. As mentioned earlier, Weindling (1932) was the first to recognize that Trichoderma spp., is a biocontrol agent and at the same time he also noticed mycoparasitism of *T. lignorum* (*viride*) hypae coiling and killing *R. solani* (Wells, 1988). Mycoparasitism is a complex mechanism that generally involves the production of a cell wall lytic enzyme. Chet *et al.* (1998) described that the mycoparasitism process involves four sequential steps: chemotropism and recognition; attachment and coiling; cell wall penetration; and digestion of host cell. Trichoderma strains detect other fungi, grow straight towards them, and sequentially produce hydrolytic cell wall degrading enzymes. Trichoderma attach to the host, and coil hyphae around the host, form appressoria on the host surface, penetrate the host cell, and collapse the host hyphae (Steyaert *et al.*, 2003). The molecular level induction of mycoparasitism was first reported in 1994 (Carsolio *et al.*, 1999), based on the study of regulation of an endochitinase-encoding gene (ech42). Ech42 was expressed during the mycoparasitic interaction between *T. harzianum* and *Rhizoctonia solani*. Another study showed that in the P1 mutant strain of *T. atroviride*, the expression of exochitinase nagI or endochitinase ech42 gene was needed to induce mycoparasitism in treatments containing purified colloidal chitin from the fungal cell walls (Vinale *et al.*, 2008). Production and regulation of lytic enzymes such as chitinases, glucanases, and proteases by *Trichoderma spp.* also play key roles in the mycoparasitism/biocontrol process (Mukherjee *et al.*, 2008).

Page
131

10. Plant growth enhancement by *Trichoderma* spp.

Trichoderma spp. are not only control pathogens, they also enhance plant growth and root development (biofertilizer) and stimulate plant defence mechanisms (Harman, 2004a). Some *Trichoderma* strains have been shown to penetrate the epidermis and establish robust and long-lasting colonization of root surfaces (Harman, 2004a). *Trichoderma* spp. have been shown to improve growth of lettuce, tomato and pepper plants (Vinale *et al.*, 2006). In a study of maize plants, several months after treatment with *Trichoderma harzianum* strain T-22, the plant roots were about twice as long when compared to untreated plants (Harman, 2004a). Cutler (1986, 1989) showed that the secondary metabolites produced by *Trichoderma koningii* (koningin A) and *Trichoderma harzianum* (6-pentylalpha pryone) act as plant growth regulators. Trichoderma spp. also produced gluconic and citric acids, decreased the soil pH, and enhanced the solubilization of phosphates, micronutrients, and mineral components such as iron, magnesium, and manganese (Benitez *et al.*, 2004; Harman *et al.*, 2004b; Vinale *et al.*, 2008).

11. Induction of plant defence by *Trichoderma* spp.

It is well documented that *Trichoderma* spp. induce gene expression of proteins in plants such as chitinase, glucanase, and peroxidase against antagonistic microbes (Yedidia *et al.*, 2003; Hanson *et al.*, 2004; Harman, 2004b). It has also been shown that pre-treatment of plants with *Trichoderma* spp. increased plant resistance to pathogen attack (Harman, 2004a). *Trichoderma* spp. are opportunistic invaders, fast growers and large spore producers. They contain cell wall degrading enzymes (e.g., celluloses, chitinases, and glucanases) and produce antibiotics (Vinale *et al.*, 2008). Moreover, the presence of *Trichoderma* spp. stimulates the induction of the Hypersensitive response, Systemic Acquired Resistance (SAR) and Induced Systemic Resistance (ISR) in plants (Benitez *et al.*, 2004; Vinale *et al.*, 2008). For example, tomato plants colonized by *T. hamatum* actively induced systemic changes in plant physiology and disease resistance (Alfano *et al.*, 2007). In a study of cucumber plants, *T. asperellum* induced a systemic response of two defence genes encoding phenylalanine and hydroperoxidase lyase and systemic accumulation of phytoalexins against *Pseudomonas syringae* pv. *lachrymans* (Yedidia *et al.*, 2003). In oil palm plants the defence gene of chitinase expression was increased in *T. harzianum* and *Ganoderma boninense* treated plants compared *to G. boninense* alone treated plants (Naher *et al.*, 2011). Several studies also showed that *Trichoderma* spp. may indirectly contribute to systemic resistance (Ahmed *et al.*, 2000; Lo *et al.*, 2000). Harman *et al.* (2004a) reported that the induction of localized or systemic resistance is an important component for plant disease control by *Trichoderma* spp. Thus, disease control by

Chapter - 13

root-colonizing *Trichoderma* spp. involves a complex interaction between the host plant, the pathogen, the biocontrol agent and several environmental factors (Harman, 2004a; Alfano *et al.*, 2007).

12. Plant root colonization by *Trichoderma* spp.

Studies of the early invading fungi *Trichoderma* spp. showed that root colonization stimulated plant defence responses such as induction of peroxidases, chitinases, β-1, 3 glucanase, phenylalanine, and hydroperoxidase lyase; activated signaling of biosynthetic pathways; and caused accumulation of low-molecular weight phytoalexins (Howell *et al.*, 2000; Yedidia *et al.*, 2003; Harman *et al.*, 2004a). Yedidia *et al.* (1999) observed the physical interaction between *T. harzianum* T-203 and a cucumber plant under the electron microscope and found that the fungus penetrated the root and grew in the epidermis and outer cortex, which stimulated increases of peroxidase and chitinase. Therefore, the interaction appears to be a symbiotic relationship in which Trichoderma lives in the nutritional niche provided by the plant, and the plant was protected from disease.

13. Production of antibiotics and secondary compounds by *Trichoderma* spp.

Secondary compounds and antibiotics produced by *Trichoderma* spp. play a vital role in antagonistic biocontrol activity (Vinale *et al.,* 2008; Ajitha and Lakshmidevi, 2010). Sivasithamparam and Ghisalberti (1998) reported that *Trichoderma* spp. produced several secondary compounds, including antibacterial and antifungal antibiotics such as polyketides, pyrones, and terpenes. Secondary metabolites, including antibiotics, that are not directly involved in natural growth, development, or reproduction and are chemically different from natural compounds may play important roles in the defence response, symbiosis, metal transport, differentiation, and stimulating or inhibiting spore formation and germination (Demain and Fang, 2000; Vinale *et al.,* 2008). Antibiotics are often associated with biocontrol activity. For example, the production of a pyrone-like antibiotic from *T. harzianum* exhibited biocontrol activity against *Ganumannomyces graminis* (Ghisalberti *et al.,* 1990). The peptide antibiotic paracelsin was the first secondary metabolite characterized in *Trichoderma* spp. (Bruckner and Graf, 1983; Bruckner *et al.,*1984). Sivasithamparam and Ghisalberti (1991) suggested that secondary metabolites produced by *Trichoderma* spp., can be grouped into three categories: (i) volatile compounds (e.g., 6-pentyl-alpha-pyrone), (ii) water-soluble compounds (e.g., heptelidic acid), and (iii) peptaibol compounds, which are linear oligopeptides composed of 12-22 amino acids that are rich in alpha-amino isobutyrate, N-acetylated at the N-terminus and have an amino alcohol group at the C-terminus.

14. Efficacy of *Trichoderma* spp. against soil-borne mycoflora

Biological control of phytopathogens is a prospective non-chemical way for disease control. *Trichoderma* species found to be most effective biocontrol under greenhouse and field conditions against many plant diseases caused by soil-borne pathogens (Srinivasa and Devi, 2014) and their efficacy highly depend upon physiological and environmental parameters such as temperature (Colussi *et al.*, 2012), pH (Romero-Arenas *et al.*, 2012), growth medium (Blaya *et al.*, 2013), light (Schmoll *et al.*, 2009), carbon and nitrogen sources (Onilude *et al.*, 2013). However, hyphal establishment, growth and biocontrol potential of *Trichoderma* greatly depend upon the biotic component interaction of various agricultural soil and all climatic zones (Bae and Knudsen, 2005) and *Trichoderma* isolates reported as successful biocontrol that retard growth of soil fungi (Keswani *et al.*, 2014).

15. *Trichoderma* as a protector of plant health

The beneficial action of *Trichoderma* spp. is not limited to fighting pathogens; they have also been shown to be opportunistic plant symbionts, enhancing systemic resistance of plants (Shoresh *et al.*, 2010), a response which is improved by ceratoplatan in family proteins (Djonović *et al.*, 2006). Perception of the signals transmitted by *Trichoderma* in the plant requires the function of a MAPK and also in the fungus itself, a MAPK signaling is crucial for full induction of systemic response in the plant (Viterbo *et al.*, 2005). By colonizing plant roots, which is significantly enhanced by swollenin (Brotman *et al.*, 2008) or invading them, they are also carried through soil and occupy new niches. This interaction with plants as well as their rhizosphere competence leads to enhanced root proliferation, better growth, and protection of the plants against toxic chemicals, against which *Trichoderma* spp. themselves show a remarkable resistance. Hence, these fungi are promising agents that can be applied for remediation of polluted soil and water by treatment of appropriate plants with spores (Harman *et al.*, 2004a).

16. Food Industry

With their long history of safe industrial scale enzyme production, *Trichoderma* spp. has also been extensively applied for production of food additives and related products (Blumenthal, 2004). Currently, various *Trichoderma* enzymes are applied to improve the brewing process (β-glucanases), as macerating enzymes in fruit juice production (pectinases, cellulases, hemicellulases), as a feed additive in livestock farming (xylanases) and for pet food. Cellulases are mainly applied in baking, malting, and grain alcohol production. However, not only enzymes but also metabolites of *Trichoderma* spp. are used as additives. One of the first products

isolated from *T. viride* was a chemical with characteristic coconut-like aroma, a 6-pentyl-α-pyrone with antibiotic properties, the production of which was constantly improved to reach concentrations of more than 7 g/L in extractive fermentation cultures in *T. atroviride* nowadays (Oda *et al.*, 2009). An interesting idea is the application of cell wall-degrading enzymes, for example of *T. harzianum*, as food preservatives because of their antifungal effect, but so far this suggestion has not found broad application. With a similar aim, *T. harzianum* mutanase can be used in toothpaste to prevent accumulation of mutan in dental plaque (Wiater *et al.*, 2005).

17. Commercialization of *Trichoderma* products

Commercialization of *Trichoderma* or biocontrol agents depends upon the screening process of biocontrol microorganism and its efficacy against pathogenic mycoflora. The first species of *Trichoderma* (*Trichoderma harzianum*) registered with EPA in 1989 for control of plant pathogens and diseases (Fravel, 2005).

Commercialization of biocontrol products is a multistep process and includes (Table - 2)

a) Isolation of microorganisms
b) Evaluation of antagonists in lab and field conditions
c) Selecting best isolate in field conditions
d) Mass production
e) Formulation
f) Delivery
g) Compatibility
h) Registration and release

18. Methods of application *Trichoderma* species Seed treatment

Seed treatment is also known as seed priming used for multiple purposes on many crops to provide inexpensive cover against wilting and rotting of planted seeds by soil-borne fungi such as *Rhizoctonia, Sclerotinia,* and *Macrophomina* species. For this purpose, mix 10 grams *Trichoderma* formulation for 1 kg of seed to per liter of cow dung slurry before sowing especially for pulses and cereal crops. *Trichoderma* multiply, reproduce and move towards the root of germinating seed where it fixes nitrogen and increases nutrients, various toxic metals and metabolites uptake and (Harman, 2006) root colonization by *Trichoderma* species promote root growth and increases resistant to abiotic stresses. *Trichoderma* seed treatment enhance chances of germination, vigor index and defense mechanism of the plant (Harman *et al.*, 2004b).

Chapter - 13

Table - 2. *Trichoderma* based commercial products against various diseases

Commercial Product/Trade name	*Trichoderma* species	Target disease	Company/ Manufacturer or Distributor
Binab	*Trichoderma* spp.	Root rot and wilt	Binab, Sweden
Anti-Fungus	*Trichoderma* spp	Root rot	Grondoonts mettingen De Ceuster, Belgium
Biofungus, Superesivit	*Trichoderma* spp.	Root rot and wilt	Bioplant, Denmark
Root Shield, Plant Shield, T-22 Planter box	*T. harzianum* T-22	Root rot	Bioworks, Geneva, USA
Tricho-X	*T. viride*	Root rot	Excel Industries Ltd., India
Biogourd	*Trichoderma viride*		Krishi Rasayan Export Pvt. Ltd., Solan (HP), India
Ecofit	*Trichoderma*		Hoechest and Schering Agro. Evo. Ltd., Mumbai, India
Trichogourd	*Trichoderma viride*		Anu Biotech international Ltd. Bangalore, India
Funginil	*Trichoderma viride*		Crop Health Bioproduct Research Centre, Gaziabad (UP), India

19. Conclusion

In 1930, Weindling first discovered the genus *Trichoderm* spp. as a biocontrol agent and since then numerous studies have demonstrated that *Trichoderma* is an effective bicontrol agent for phytopathogenic microorganisms (Harman, 1996). A biocontrol program is only established when the bicontrol agent can successfully manage the interaction between the host plant and pathogen. The ability of *Trichoderma* to successfully manage this interaction has been well established. The fungi have also been demonstrated to enhance the defence responses in plants. Thus, as an effective biocontrol agent the use of *Trichoderma*.

Chapter - 13

20. References

1) Ahmed, A.S., C.P. Sanchez and M.E. Candela. 2000. Evaluation of induction of systemic resistance in pepper plants (*Capsicum annum*) to *Phytopthora capsici* using *Trichoderma harzianum* and its relation with capsidiol accumulation. *Eur. J. Plant Pathol.*, 106: 817 - 829.

2) Alfano, G., L. M. Lewis Ivey, C. Cakir, J. I. B. Bos, S. A. Miller, V. L. Madden Kamoun and J. A. H. Hoitink. 2007. Systemic modulation of gene S. expression in tomato by *Trichoderma hamatum* 382. *Biological Control*, 97: 429 - 437.

3) Aluko, M. O., and Hering, T. F. 1970. The mechanism associated with the antagonistic relationship between *Corticium solani* and *Gliocladium virens*. *Trans. Br. Mycol. Soc.* 55: 173 - 179.

4) Alvindia, D. G., Hirooka, Y. 2011. Identification of *Clonostachys* and *Trichoderma* spp. from banana fruit surfaces by cultural, morphological and molecular methods. *Mycology*, 2, 109-115.

5) Ajitha, P. S and N. Lakshmedevi. 2010. Effect of volatile and von-volatile compounds from *Trichoderma* spp. Against *Colletotrichum capsica* incitant of anthracnose on Bell peppers. *Nature and Sci.*, 8: 265 - 296.

6) Alizadeh, H., Behboudi, K., Ahmadzadeh, M., Javan-Nikkhah, M., Zamioudis, C., Pieterse, C. M. J and Bakker, P. A. H. M. 2013. Induced systemic resistance in cucumber and *Arabidopsis thaliana* by the combination of *Trichoderma harzianum* Tr6 and *Pseudomonas* sp. Ps14. *Biological Control*, 65: 14 - 23.

7) Bae, Y. S and Knudsen, G. R. 2005. Soil microbial biomass influence on growth and biocontrol efficacy of *Trichoderma harzianum*. *Biological Control*, 32: 236 - 242.

8) Benitez, T., A. M. Rincon, M. C. Limon and A. C. Codon. 2004. Biocontrol mechanism of *Trichoderma* strains. *International Microbiology*, 7: 249 - 260.

9) Bissett, J., Szakacs, G., Nolan, C.A., Druzhinina, I., Gradinger, C., Kubicek, C.P., 2003. New species of *Trichoderma* from Asia. *Canadian Journal of Botany*, 81: 570-586.

10) Bliss, D. E. 1951. The destruction of *Armillaria mellea* in citrus soils. *Phytopathology*, 41: 665 - 683.

11) Brimner, T.A., Boland, G.J., 2003. A review of the non-target effects of fungi used to biologically control plant diseases. *Agriculture, Ecosystems & Environment*, 100: 3 - 16.

Chapter - 13

12) Brotman, Y., Landau, U., Cuadros-Inostroza, Á., Takayuki, T., Fernie, A. R., Chet, I., Viterbo, A and Willmitzer, L. 2013. *Trichoderma* - plant root colonization: escaping early plant defense responses and activation of the antioxidant machinery for saline stress tolerance. *PLoS Pathogens*, 9: e1003221.

13) Brotman, Y., Briff, E., Viterbo, A., Chet, I. 2008. Role of swollenin, an expansin-like protein from *Trichoderma*, in plant root colonization. *Plant Physiology*, 147: 779 - 789.

14) Blumenthal, C. Z. 2004. Production of toxic metabolites in *Aspergillus niger*, *Aspergillus oryzae*, and *Trichoderma reesei*: justification of mycotoxin testing in food grade enzyme preparations derived from the three fungi. *Regulatory Toxicology and Pharmacology*, 39: 214 - 228.

15) Blaya, J., López-Mondéjar, R., Lloret, E., Pascual, J.A., Ros, M., 2013. Changes induced by *Trichoderma harzianum* in suppressive compost controlling *Fusarium* wilt. *Pesticide Biochemistry and Physiology*, 107: 112-119.

16) Carsolio, C., N. Benhamou, S. Haran, C. Cortes, A. Gutierrez, I. Chet and A. Herrera-Estrella. 1999. Role of the *Trichoderma harzianum* endochitinase gene, *ech42*, in mycoparasitism. *Appl. Environ. Microbiol.*, 65: 929 - 935.

17) Chaudhari, P. J., Shrivastava, P and Khadse, A. C. 2011. Substrate evaluation for mass cultivation of *Trichoderma viride*. *Asiatic Journal of Biotechnology Resources*, 2: 441 - 446.

18) Chaverri, P., Gazis, R. O., Samuels, G. J. 2011. *Trichoderma amazonicum*, a new endophytic species on *Hevea brasiliensis*and *H. guianensis* from the Amazon basin. *Mycologia*, 103: 139 - 151.

19) Chet, I., N. Benhamou and S. Harman. 1998. Mycoparasitism and lytic enzymes. In: *Trichoderma and Gliocladium* Vol. 2. (Eds.): G.E. Harman and C.P. Kubick. London, Taylor and Francis. pp. 153-172.

20) Colussi, F., Garcia, W., Rosseto, F.R., de Mello, B.L., de Oliveira Neto, M., Polikarpov, I., 2012. Effect of pH and temperature on the global compactness, structure, and activity of cellobiohydrolase Cel7A from *Trichoderma harzianum*. *European Biophysics Journal*, 41: 89-98.

21) Demain, A. L. and A. Fang. 2000. The natural functions of secondary metabolites. *Advances in Biochem. Engineer. Biotechnol.*, 69: 1 - 39.

22) Djonović, S., Pozo, M. J., Dangott, L. J., Howell, C. R and Kenerley, C. M. 2006. Sm1, a proteinaceous elicitor secreted by the biocontrol fungus *Trichoderma virens* induces plant defense responses and systemic resistance. *Molecular Plant-Microbe Interactions*, 19: 838 - 853.

23) Dubey, S. C., Bhavani, R and Singh, B. 2009. Development of Pusa 5SD for seed dressing and Pusa Biopellet 10G for soil application formulations of *Trichoderma harzianum* and their evaluation for integrated management of dry root rot of mungbean (*Vigna radiata*). *Biological Control*, 50: 231-242.

24) El-Mohamedy, R.S.R., Alla, M.A., 2013. Bio-priming seed treatment for biological control of soil borne fungi causing root rot of green bean (*Phaseolus vulgaris* L.). *Journal of Agricultural Technology*, 9: 589-599.

25) Fravel, D. R. 2005. Commercialization and Implementation of biocontrol. *Annual Review of Phytopathology*, 43: 337-359.

26) Gams, W., and Bisset, J. 1998. Morphology and identification of *Trichoderma*. Pages 3 - 34 in: *Trichoderma & Gliocladium*. Vol. 1. G. E. Harman and C. P. Kubicek, eds. Taylor and Francis, London.

27) Gao, L., Sun, M. H., Liu, X. Z and Che, Y. S. 2007. Effects of carbon concentration and carbon to nitrogen ratio on the growth and sporulation of several biocontrol fungi. *Mycological Research*, 111: 87 - 92.

28) Ghisalberti, E. L., M. J. Narbey, M. M. Dewan and K. Sivasithamparam. 1990. Variability among strains of *Trichoderma harzianum* in their ability to reduce take-all and to produce pyrones. *Plant and Soil*, 121: 287 - 291.

29) Grinyer, J., McKay, M., Nevalainen, H and Herbert, B. R. 2004. Fungal proteomics: initial mapping of biological control strain *Trichoderma harzianum*. *Current Genetics*, 45: 163-169.

30) Gupta, S and Dikshit, A. 2010. Biopesticides: An ecofriendly approach for pest control. *Journal of Biopesticides*, 3: 186 - 188.

31) Gveroska, B and Ziberoski, J. 2012. *Trichoderma harzianum* as a biocontrol agent against *Alternaria alternata* on tobacco. *Applied Technologies and Innovations*, 7: 67 - 76.

32) Harman, G. E. 2000. Myths and dogmas of biocontrol: Changes in perceptions derived from research on *Trichoderma harzianum* T- 22. *Plant Disease*, 84: 377 - 393.

33) Harman, G. E., C. R. Howell, A. Viterbo, I. Chet and M. Lorito. 2004a. *Trichoderma* species - opportunistic, avirulent plant symbionts. *Nature Rev. Microbiol.*, 2: 43 - 56.

34) Harmam, G. E., R. Petzoldt, A. Comis and J. Chen. 2004b. Interactions between *Trichoderma harzianum* strain T22 and maize inbred line M017 and effects of these interactions on diseases by *Pythium ultimum* and *Collectotrichum graminicola*. *Phytopathol.*, 94: 147 - 153.

35) Hanson, L. E and C. R. Howell. 2004. Elicitors of plant defence responses from biocontrol strains of *Trichoderma virens*. *Phytopathol.*, 94: 171 - 176.

36) Harman, G. E., Howell, C. R., Viterbo, A., Chet, I., Lorito, M., 2004a. *Trichoderma* species - opportunistic, avirulent plant symbionts. *Nature Reviews Microbiology*, 2: 43 - 56.

37) Harman, G. E. 2006. Overview of mechanisms and uses of *Trichoderma* spp. *Phytopathology*, 96: 190 - 194.

38) Harman, G. E., Herrera-Estrella, A. H., Horwitz, B. A and Lorito, M. 2012. Special issue: *Trichoderma* - from basic biology to biotechnology. *Microbiology*, 158: 1 - 2.

39) Harman, G. E., Lorito, M and Lynch, J. M. 2004b. Uses of *Trichoderma* spp. to alleviate or remediate soil and water pollution. *Advances in Applied Microbiology*, 56: 313 - 330.

40) Haggag, K. H. E and El-Gamal, N. G. 2012. *In vitro* study on *Fusarium solani* and *Rhizoctonia solani* isolates causing the damping off and root rot diseases in tomatoes. *Nature and Science*, 10: 16 - 25.

41) Hjeljord, L. G., A. Stensvand and A. Tronsmo. 2000. Effect of temperature and nutrient stress on the capacity of commercial *Trichoderma* products to control *Botrytis cinerea* and *Mucor piriformis* in greenhouse strawberries. *Biological Control*, 19: 149 - 160.

42) Howell, C. R. 2003. Mechanisms employed by *Trichoderma* species in the biological control of plant diseases: the history and evolution of current concepts. *Plant Disease*, 87: 4 - 10.

43) Jaklitsch, W. M., Samuels, G. J., Dodd, S. L., Lu, B. S and Druzhinina, I. S. 2006. *Hypocrearufa/ Trichoderma viride*: a reassessment, and description of five closely related species with and without warted conidia. *Studies in Mycology*, 56: 135 - 177.

44) Kumar, S. 2013. *Trichoderma*: a biological weapon for managing plant diseases and promoting sustainability. *International Journal of Agriculture Science and Medical Veterinary*, 1: 106 - 121.

45) Küçük, Ç and Kivanç, M. 2003. Isolation of *Trichoderma* spp. and determination of their antifungal, biochemical and physiological features. *Turkish Journal of Biology*, 27: 247 - 253.

46) Kim, C. S., Park, M. S., Kim, S. C., Maekawa, N and Yu, S. H. 2012. Identification of *Trichoderma*, a competitor of shiitake mushroom (*Lentinula edodes*), and competition between *Lentinula edodes* and *Trichoderma* species in Korea. *The Plant Pathology Journal*, 28: 137 - 148.

47) Keswani, C., Mishra, S., Sarma, B. K., Singh, S. P and Singh, H. B. 2014. Unraveling the efficient applications of secondary metabolites of various *Trichoderma* spp. *Applied Microbiology and Biotechnology*, 98: 533 - 544.

48) Latifian, M., Hamidi Esfahani, Z and Barzegar, M. 2007. Evaluation of culture conditions for cellulase production by two *Trichoderma reesei* mutants under solid-state fermentation conditions. *Bioresource Technology*, 98: 3634 - 3637.

49) Lu, B., Druzhinina, I. S., Fallah, P., Chaverri, P., Gradinger, C., Kubicek, C. P., Samuels, G. J. 2004. *Hypocrea/ Trichoderma* species with pachybasium-like conidiophores: teleomorphs for *T. minutisporum* and *T. polysporum* and their newly discovered relatives. *Mycologia*, 96: 310 - 342.

50) Manjunatha, S. V., Naik, M. K., Khan, M. F. R and Goswami, R. S. 2013. Evaluation of bio-control agents for management of dry root rot of chickpea caused by *Macrophomina phaseolina. Crop Protection*, 45: 118 – 125.

51) Mukherjee, K. P, C. S. Nautiyal and A. N. Mukhopadhyay. 2008. Molecular mechanisms of plant and microbe coexistence. Springer, Heidelberg.

52) Naher, L., C. L. Ho, S. G. Tan, U. K. Yusuf and F. Abdullah. 2011. Cloning transcripts encoding chitinases from *Elaeisguine ensis* Jacq. and their expression profiles in response to fungal infections. *Physiol. Mol. Plant Pathol.*, 76: 96 - 103.

53) Oda, S., Isshiki, K and Ohashi, S. 2009. Production of 6-pentyl-α-pyrone with *Trichoderma atroviride* and its mutant in a novel extractive liquid-surface immobilization (Ext-LSI) system. *Process Biochemistry*, 44: 625 - 630.

54) Onilude, A. A., Adebayo-Tayo, B. C., Odeniyi, A. O., Banjo, D and Garuba, E. O. 2013. Comparative mycelial and spore yield by *Trichoderma viride* in batch and fed-batch cultures. *Annals of Microbiology*, 63: 547 - 553.

55) Papavizas, G. C. 1985. *Trichodema* and *Gliocladium*: Biology, ecology and potential for biocontrol. *Ann. Rev. Phytopathol.*, 22: 23 - 54.

56) Reese, E. T. 1976. History of the cellulose program at the U.S. Army Natick development center. *Biotechnol. Bioeng. Sympos.*, 6: 9 - 20.

57) Romero-Arenas, O., Huato, M. A. D., Trevintilde, I. H., Lezama, J. F. C. P., García, A. A and Arellano, A. D. V. 2012. Effect of pH on growth of the mycelium of *Trichoderma viride* and *Pleurotus ostreatus* in solid cultivation mediums. *African Journal of Agricultural Research*, 7: 4724 - 4730.

58) Samanta, S., Basu, A., Halder, U. C and Sen, S. K. 2012. Characterization of *Trichoderma reesei* endoglucanase ii expressed heterologously in *Pichia pastoris* for better biofinishing and biostoning. *Journal of Microbiology*, 50: 518 - 525.

59) Samuels, G. J., Dodd, S. L., Gams, W., Castlebury, L. A and Petrini, O. 2002. *Trichoderma* species associated with the green mold epidemic of commercially grown *Agaricus bisporus*. *Mycologia*, 94: 146 - 170.

60) Samuels, G. J. 2006. *Trichoderma*: systematics, the sexual state and ecology. *Phytopathology*, 96: 195 - 206.

61) Santoro, P. H., Cavaguchi, S. A., Alexandre, T. M., Zorzetti, J and Neves, P. M. O. J. 2014. *In vitro* sensitivity of antagonistic *Trichoderma atroviride* to herbicides. *Brazilian Archives of Biology and Technology*, 57: 238 – 243.

62) Schmoll, M., Schuster, A., Silva, R. N and Kubicek, C. P. 2009. The G-Alpha protein GNA3 of *Hypocrea jecorina* (Anamorph *Trichoderma reesei*) regulates cellulase gene expression in the presence of light. *Eukaryotic Cell*, 8: 410 - 420.

63) Singh, V., Joshi, B. B., Awasthi, S. K and Srivastava, S. N. 2008. Eco-friendly management of red rot disease of sugarcane with *Trichoderma* strains. *Sugar Tech.*, 10: 158 - 161.

64) Sivasithamparam, K and E. L. Ghisalberti. 1998. Secondary metabolism in *Trichoderma* and *Gliocladium*. In: *Trichoderma and Gliocladium*. (Eds.): G.E. Harman and C. P. Kubicek. Taylor and Francis, London, pp. 139-192.

65) Steyaert, J. M, H. J. Ridgway, Y. Elad and A. Stewart. 2003. Genetic basis of mycoparasitism: A mechanism of biological control by species of *Trichoderma*. *J. Crop. Horticul. Sci.*, 31: 281 - 291.

66) Srinivasa, N and Devi, T. P. 2014. Separation and identification of antifungal compounds from *Trichoderma* species BY GC-MS and their bio-efficacy against soil-borne pathogens. *Quarterly Journal of Life Sciences*, 11: 255 - 257.

67) Shoresh, M., Harman, G. E and Mastouri, F. 2010. Induced systemic resistance and plant responses to fungal biocontrol agents. *Annual Review of Phytopathology*, 48: 21 - 43.

68) Vinale, F., K. Sivasithamparam, L. E. Ghisalberti, R. Marra, L. S. Woo and M. Lorito. 2008. *Trichoderma* – plant pathogen interactions. *Soil. Biol. Biochem.*, 40: 1 - 10.

69) Vinale, F., R. Marra, F. Scale, E. L. Ghisalberti, M. Lorito and K. Sivasithamparam. 2006. Major secondary metabolites produced by two commercial *Trichoderma* strains active different phytopathogens. *Letter in Applied Microbiol.*, 43: 143 - 148.

70) Viterbo, A., Harel, M., Horwitz, B. A., Chet, I and Mukherjee, P. K. 2005. *Trichoderma* Mitogen-activated protein kinase signaling is involved in induction of plant systemic resistance. *Applied and Environmental Microbiology*, 71: 6241 - 6246.

71) Wiater, A., Szczodrak, J and Pleszczyńska, M. 2005. Optimization of conditions for the efficient production of mutan in *Streptococcal* cultures and post-culture liquids. *Acta Biologica Hungarica*, 56: 137 - 150.

72) Weindling, R. 1932. *Trichoderma lignorum* as a parasite of other soil fungi. *Phytopathology*, 22: 837 - 845.

73) Weindling, R. 1934. Studies on lethal principle effective in the parasitic action of *Trichoderma lignorum* on *Rhizoctinia solani* and other soil fungi. *Phytopathol.*, 24: 1153 - 1179.

74) Wells, H. D., Bell, D. K and Jaworski, C. A. 1972. Efficacy of *Trichoderma harzianum* as a biocontrol for *Sclerotium rolfsii*. *Phytopathology*, 62: 442 - 447.

75) Wells, D. H. 1988. *Trichoderma* as a biocontrol agent. In: *Biocontrol and Plant Diseases*. (Eds.): K.G. Mukerji and K. L. Garg. CRC press, Florida, pp. 73.

76) Yedidia, I., N. Benhamou and I. Chet. 1999. Induction of defence responses in cucumber plants (*Cucumis sativus* L.) by the biocontrol agent *Trichoderma harzianum*. *Appl. Environ. Microbiol.*, 65: 10061 - 1070.

77) Yedidia, I., Shoresh, M., Kerem, Z., Benhamou, N., Kapulnik, Y., Chet, I., 2003. Concomitant induction of systemic resistance to *Pseudomonas syringae* pv. *lachrymans* in cucumber by *Trichoderma asperellum* (T-203) and accumulation of phytoalexins. *Applied and Environmental Microbiology*, 69: 7343 - 7353.

78) Zhang, C. L., Druzhinina, I. S., Kubicek, C. P and Xu, T. 2005. *Trichoderma* biodiversity in China: evidence for a North to South distribution of species in East Asia. *FEMS Microbiology Letters*, 251: 251 - 257.

79) Zhang, C. L., Liu, S. P., Lin, F. C., Kubicek, C. P and Druzhinina, I. S. 2007. *Trichoderma taxi* sp. nov., an endophytic fungus from Chinese yew *Taxus mairei*. *FEMS Microbiology Letters*, 270: 90 - 96.

80) Zhang, J., Howell, C. R and Starr, J. L. 1996. Suppression of *Fusarium* colonization of cotton roots and *Fusarium* wilt by seed treatments with *Gliocladium virens* and *Bacillus subtilis*. *Biocontrol Sci. Technol.* 6: 175 - 187.

Scientific Advancements in Current Agricultural Research
ISBN: 978-81-947154-7-4
First Edition; 2020
Chapter – 14, Page: 144 - 152

14

IMPACT OF POTASH SOLUBILIZING MICROORGANISM FOR SUSTAINABLE AGRICULTURE

G. Kumaresan, J. Jayachitra and P. Sivasakthivelan

Department of Agricultural Microbiology, Faculty of Agriculture, Annamalai University, Annamalai Nagar, Tamil Nadu, India

Abstract

Potassium (K) is considered as an essential nutrient and a major constituent within all living cells. Naturally, soils contain K in larger amounts than any other nutrients; however, most of the K is unavailable for plant uptake. Application of chemical fertilizers has a considerably negative impact on environmental sustainability. It is known that potassium solubilizing bacteria (KSB) can solubilize K-bearing minerals and convert the insoluble K to soluble forms of K available to plant uptake. Countless soil microscopic organisms, for example, *Acidoithiobacillus ferrooxidans, Paenibacillus* spp., *Bacillus mucilaginosus, B. edaphicus*, and *B. circulans*, have ability to solubilize K minerals like biotite, muscovite, feldspar, mica, iolite, and orthoclase. KSB are normally present in every one of the soil, in spite of the fact that their number, assorted variety, and capacity for K solubilization differ which rely on the soil and climatic conditions. Despite that, KSB are the most essential microscopic organisms for solubilizing K minerals which demonstrate viable association amongst soil and plant frameworks. These microbes can be utilized productively as a wellspring of K-fertilizer for managing crop generation and keeping up soil K. Subsequently, generation and administration of organic manures containing KSB can scatter K inadequacy particularly in paddy field or zones where plants are normal for K and are likewise an approach to accomplish the objectives of the practical farming. This article shows a diagram of flow patterns and difficulties

on the KSB, components, and their part in plant development advancement and in the end gives a few viewpoints for study on K in agriculture.

Keywords: Potassium solubilizing bacteria (KSB), Biofertilizer and Mineral bearing potassium.

1. Introduction

Potassium (K) is an essential nutrient that plays important roles for plant growth and development, such as activating enzymes, maintaining turgor, transporting of nutrient, and protecting plant from disease and insects. It is a key element in many physiological and biochemical processes. Microbial community impacts fertility of soil by means of various activities like dissolution, enhancing the availability of nutrients, and improving the nutrient acquisition (Parmar and Sindhu, 2013). As of late, potassium solubilizing microbes have pulled in consideration of researchers as soil inoculant to improve the development of plant and yield. These microorganisms are powerful in discharging K from inorganic and insoluble pools of aggregate soil K by solubilization process (Sindhu *et al.,* 2014). K solubilization is performed by an extensive range of saprophytic bacteria, fungal strains, and actinomycetes. There are solid confirmations that soil bacteria are equipped for changing soil K to the forms accessible to plant (Saiyad *et al.,* 2015). Many bacteria such as *Acidothiobacillus ferrooxidans, Paenibacillus* spp., *Bacillus mucilaginosus, B. edaphicus,* and *B. circulans* have capacity to solubilize K minerals (e.g., biotite, feldspar, illite, muscovite, orthoclase, and mica). KSB are usually present in all soils, although their number, diversity and ability for K solubilization vary depending upon the soil and climatic conditions.

The microbial solubilization of K is strongly affected by pH, the bacterial strains utilized, oxygen, and sort of K-bearing minerals; in fact, moderate alkalinity supports the solubilization of silicate. Silicate bacteria were found to dissolve potassium, silicon and aluminium from insoluble minerals. It has been reported that most of potassium in soil exists in the form of silicate minerals. The potassium is made available to plants when the minerals are slowly weathered or solubilized In general, black soils are high, red soils medium and lateritic soils lows in available K. Lateritic, shallow red and black soils have been found to show decline in K fertility over the years under intensive cultivation and imbalanced fertilizer application. Since K is a costly nutrient, India ranks 4th in consumption of potassium fertilizers. On an average 1.7 million tons of K is being imported annually (Anonymous, 2003). Therefore, the current chapter to discuss about the influence of efficient mineral potassium solublizing bacteria on growth and yield of agricultural crop.

Chapter -14

2. Bacteria-Soil-Plant Interactions

Soils are complex blends of minerals, water, air, organic matter, and billions of organisms, and the progressions occurring in its organization are called biogeochemical changes. Soil fertility alludes to the limit of the soil to supply basic plant nutrients, for example, N, P, K, and iron (Fe), while the inorganic types of these minerals are made by microorganisms amid mineralization process (Zhao *et al.* 2016). In the soil, it is conceivable to discover different sorts of microorganisms, for example, bacteria, fungi, actinomycetes, protozoa, and algae, which microscopic organisms are by a wide margin

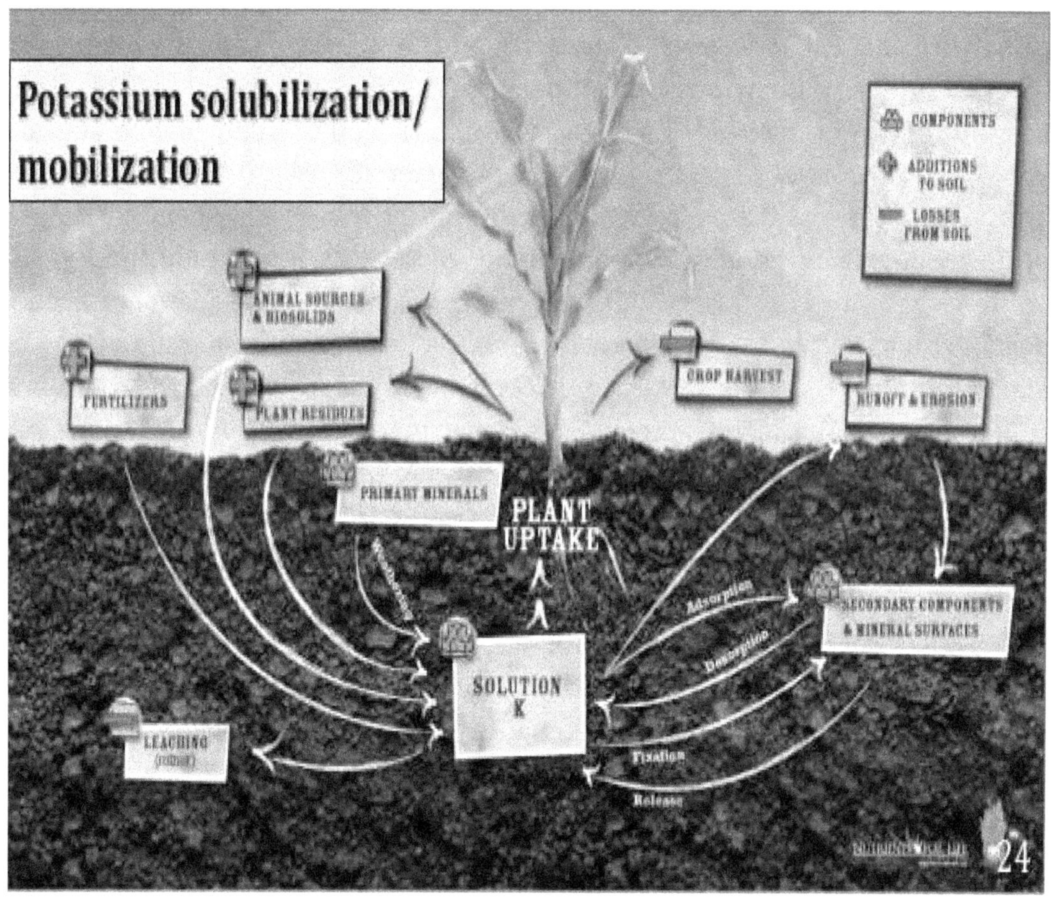

Figure – 1: Bacteria-Soil-Plant Interactions

the most well-known (i.e., ~ 95%). There are an several unique bacterial species, most of which presently can't seem to be even identified properly, and every species has its own specific importance and abilities. The number and variability of bacteria are affected by the soil structure, for example, organic carbon, temperature, moisture, and electrical conductivity, and different chemicals, and additionally by the number

and kinds of plants found in those soils. Moreover, the majority of which underlying around plant roots in rhizosphere (Dessaux *et al.,* 2009). This is a direct result of occurrence of nutritional substances including organic acids, sugars, amino acids, and other small molecules from exudates produced by roots. The bacteria may influence plant development in one of three different ways. The communication might be helpful (e.g. plant development advancing rhizobacteria and predatory enemies of herbivores), harmful (e.g. pathogens and herbivorous insects), or neutral for plant, and at times the effect of microbes may differ based on changes in soil conditions (Cheng *et al.,* 2010).

The bacteria that give a few advantages to plants are (I) those that form nodules on host plant roots (symbiotic relationship) and fix nitrogen; (ii) those that don't have any harmful effect on host plant while multiplying inside the plant tissues; (iii) those that have potential of competitiveness for their survivability in rhizosphere and surface of plant roots; and (iv) those that occur in soil in free living condition. In farming, useful microbes are generally characterized with their tendency of colonization in roots of plants following seed priming or seed treatment and improve plant development by expanding submergence of seeds, plant weight, and yield of crops. In spite of the constrained information of soil bacteria and plant connections, some of these bacteria are utilized economically as aides to farming practice. These bacteria comprise *Burkholderia cepacia, Delftia acidovorans, Paenibacillus macerans, Pantoea agglomerans, Pseudomonas* spp., *P. aureofaciens, P. chlororaphis, P. fluorescens, P. solanacearum, Bacillus* spp., *B. mucilaginous, B. pumilus, B. subtilis, B. amyloliquefaciens, B. fimus, B. licheniformis, B. megaterium, Agrobacterium radiobacter, Azospirillum brasilense, A. lipoferum, Azotobacter chroococcum, P. syringae, Serratia entomophila, Streptomyces* spp., *S. griseoviridis* and *S. lydicus.* Generally, plant-advantageous bacteria help the plant development with two systems: (I) in direct mechanism by either aiding in acquisition of resources (N, P, Fe, and other essential nutrients) or directing levels of plant hormone or (II) in backhanded activity components by diminishing the pernicious impacts of different pathogens on the development and yield of plants as bio-control specialists. Till date, there are several studies that have been conducted in both pot and field experiments with significant contributions of plant growth-promoting bacteria that benefit to plant in various modes of aspects such as nutrient acquisition, growth, yield, and useful attributes related to crop productivity and soil health.

3. Potassium Solubilizing Bacteria (KSB)

Microbial community impacts fertility of soil by means of various activities like dissolution, enhancing the availability of nutrients, and improving the nutrient

acquisition (Parmar and Sindhu, 2013). As of late, potassium solubilizing microbes have pulled in consideration of researchers as soil inoculant to improve the development of plant and yield. These microorganisms are powerful in discharging K from inorganic and insoluble pools of aggregate soil K by solubilization process (Sindhu *et al.*, 2014). K solubilization is performed by an extensive range of saprophytic bacteria, fungal strains, and actinomycetes. There are solid confirmations that soil bacteria are equipped for changing soil K to the forms accessible to plant (Saiyad *et al.*, 2015). The bacteria expanding the general execution of plants by giving for the most part dissolvable K to plants in various production systems are categorized as plant growth-promoting bacteria. There is an impressive population of KSB in soil and rhizosphere of plants. These incorporate both aerobic and anaerobic isolates in that the most frequent KSB in soil are aerobic. An extensively higher concentration of KSB is generally found in the rhizosphere in comparison with non-rhizosphere soil (Padma and Sukumar, 2015). Solubilization of K by KSB from insoluble and settled forms is an important aspect as regards K accessibility in soils. Bacterial isolates having K-solubilizing potential can be screened by using modified Aleksandrov medium which is mainly based on halo zone formation surrounding the bacterial colonies as shown in Fig. 1 (Rajawat *et al.*, 2016). The capacity to solubilize the silicate rocks by *B. mucilaginosus*, *B. circulanscan*, *B. edaphicus*, *Burkholderia*, *A. ferrooxidans*, *Arthrobacter* sp., *Enterobacter hormaechei*, *Paenibacillus mucilaginosus*, *P. frequentans*, *Cladosporium*, *Aminobacter*, *Sphingomonas*, *Burkholderia*, and *Paenibacillus glucanolyticus* has been described. Amongst the soil bacterial groups, *B. mucilaginosus*, *B. edaphicus*, and *B. circulans* have been explained as effective K solubilizers (Table - 1). The microbial solubilization of K is strongly affected by pH, the bacterial strains utilized, oxygen, and sort of K-bearing minerals; in fact, moderate alkalinity supports the solubilization of silicate (Sheng and Huang 2001).

Table1. Various predominant organic acids produced by potassium solubilizing bacteria

KSMs	K source used	Reference
B. mucilaginosus	Mica and soil	Basak and Biswas 2010
B. edaphicus	K-deficient soil	Sheng 2005
B. mucilaginosus	Soil	Han and Lee 2005
B. megaterium	Muscovite and biotite	Zarjani et al. 2013
Arthrobacter spp.	Muscovite or biotite micas	Zarjani et al. 2013
B. circulanscan	Silicate mineral	Lian et al. 2002
A. terreus and A. niger	Feldspar	Prajapati et al. 2012
Penicillium spp.	Muscovite	Crawford et al. 2000
E. hormaechei (KSB-8)	Feldspar	Prajapati et al. 2013
Paenibacillus mucilaginosus	F-feldspar, kaolinite, montmorillonite	Liu et al. 2012; Hu et al. 2006
P. frequentans, Cladosporium	K-bearing minerals	Argelis et al. 1993
Aminobacter, Sphingomonas, Burkholderia	K-bearing minerals	Uroz et al. 2007

4. Action Mechanisms of KSB in Solubilizing K

In present time there is small evidence accessible on K solubilization using KSB, which showed systems of silicate mineral dissolution to pass K to enhancing the growth and yield of various plants. Diminishing pH by means of produced organic acids and protons by KSB, expanding complex formation of cations by bounding to K, and acidolysis of encompassing region of KSB are some known activity components of KSB in process of K solubilization (Maurya *et al.*, 2014). As happens on account of P solubilization, major system of K mineral solubilizations also have similar activity of organic and inorganic acids released by KSBs. Since organic acids are also supplemented by chelation, complex lysis, acidolysis, and exchange responses which are main means attributed to their translation in soluble form of K. The kinds of numerous organic acids that are generated by microbial strains

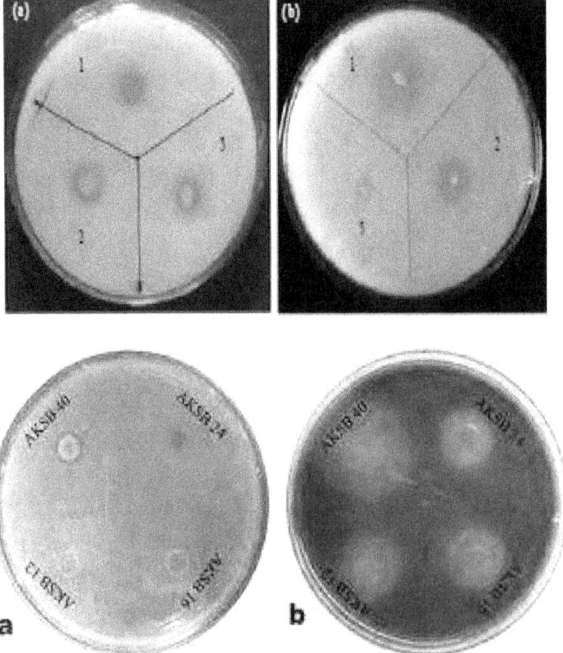

Figure – 1: Potash solubilizing capacity of certain bacterial strains

5. Effect of KSB on Crop Production

Availability of high-yielding varieties of crop and the raised intensification of agriculture, the soils are becoming depleted in K stock at a quicker rate. Microbial inoculants ready to release K from silicate have the impact on plant development parameters, yield, and K take-up through plants under both pot and field conditions (Meena *et al.* 2014). Earlier reports suggest inoculation with KSB showed

advantageous impacts on growth of cotton and rape, eggplant, pepper and cucumber, peanut, maize, sorghum, wheat, sudan grass, sorghum, and tomato. Studies suggests that the application of KSB as biofertilizers for agriculture enhancement will result into decreased use of agrochemicals and help sustainable crop production (Archana *et al.* 2012).

6. Potentialities and Challenges of KSB in Industry

KSB increases weathering process of K minerals; particularly once in direct contact with mineral surfaces through various action means. Efforts have been made to use of K-mobilizing bacteria for solubilizing K from different K-bearing minerals (Saha *et al.,* 2016) and therefore to increase plant nutrition. In spite of the fact that KSB could be a substitute and reasonable innovation to dissolve insoluble K sources into soluble forms, their application in farming practice is still avoided due to many factors. For instance, absence of information about biofertilizer amongst the farmers, moderate impact of the K biofertilizer on crop yield, low curiosity in scientific group on the advancement of K biofertilizer techniques, microbial deposition banks not yet established for KSB particularly because of this loss of proficient strains developed by scientists, and inadequacy in innovation in regard to carrier sustainability and product formulations are a portion of the real imperatives and constraints of the industry, which are expected to be improved soon.

7. Conclusions

Minerals bearing K showed leading place in the Earth's crust contributing K fertilization for crop plants. Plants acquired the K supply from soil solution that contains available K. Subsequent to this uptake, K is released into the soil from insoluble minerals, but it is smaller as per the requirement of plants, because the amount of soluble K in the soil solution is very low and K is relatively immobile in the soil. Hence, to meet up requirements of plant, K-fertilizers should be used, which are a current exercise to provide accessible K in widespread agricultural systems (Zhang *et al.,* 2013). Due to the higher price of these fertilizers, extended application causes enhanced cost of inputs. The farmers face many direct or indirect problems like decline in the agricultural output, and multiple environmental constrains due to having heavy metal accumulation in soil and plant system. These toxic chemicals accumulate into the fruits and vegetables and at last human body. It has been notable that the utilization of KSB can be a promising strategy to solubilize K from soil and convert it into accessible form for plants, bringing about advancement of plant development and limiting the use of K-fertilizers. Solubilization of K is performed by numerous bacterial strains like *B. mucilaginosus, B. edaphicus, B. circulans, Pseudomonas, Burkholderia, Acidithiobacillus ferrooxidans,* and *Paenibacillus* spp. Earlier, researches

well explained that by excreting organic acids KSB were capable to release K from various insoluble sources of K-minerals. Amongst achievement of KSB in making K accessible to plant, production of organic acids is major means, which can either directly increase K-releasing ability by either a proton- or ligand-mediated mechanism, or they can also indirectly increase release of K by the development of complexes in solution with insoluble sources of K. Hence, the use of KSB as biofertilizer not only enhances growth and yield of plant but also reduces the application of agrochemicals causing eco-friendly crop production.

8. References

1) Amaral FP, Pankievicz VCS, Arisi ACM, de Souza EM, Pedrosa F, Stacey G. (2016). Differential growth responses of Brachypodiumdistachyon genotypes to inoculation with plant growth promoting rhizobacteria. *Plant Mol Biol.* 90(6): 689 - 697.

2) Anonymous. (2003). Agricultural Statistics at a Glance, Ministry of Agriculture Cooperation, New Delhi, pp.51-53. 3. Bertsch, P. M. and Thomas, G. W. (1985). Potassium status of temperature region soils." In: Munson, R. D. (Ed.) Potassium in agriculture ASA, CSSA and SSSP, Madison, WI, pp.131-162

3) Archana DS, Nandish MS, Savalagi VP, Alagawadi AR. (2012). Screening of Potassium solubilizing bacteria (KSB) for plant growth promotional activity. *BIOINFOLET,* 9(4): 627 – 630.

4) Basak BB and Biswas DR. (2010). Co-inoculation of potassium solubilizing and nitrogen fixing bacteria on solubilization of waste mica and their effect on growth promotion and nutrient acquisition by a forage crop. *Biol. Fert. Soils,* 46(6): 641 –648.

5) Cheng Z, McConkey BJ and Glick BR. (2010). Proteomic studies of plant - bacterial interactions. *Soil Biol. Biochem.,* 42(10): 1673 – 1684.

6) Dessaux Y, Hinsinger P and Lemanceau P. (2009). Rhizosphere: so many achievements and even more challenges. *Plant Soil,* 321(1): 1 – 3.

7) Han HS and Lee KD. (2005). Phosphate and potassium solubilizing bacteria effect on mineral uptake, soil availability and growth of eggplant. *Res. J. Agric. Boil. Sci.,* 1(2): 176 – 180.

8) Liu D, Lian B and Dong H. (2012). Isolation of *Paenibacillus* sp. and assessment of its potential for enhancing mineral weathering. *Geomicrobiol. J.,* 29(5): 413 - 421

9) Maurya BR, Meena VS and Meena OP. (2014). Influence of Inceptisol and Alfisol's potassium solubilizing bacteria (KSB) isolates on release of K from waste mica. *Vegetos,* 27(1): 181 – 187.

Chapter - 14

10) Meena VS, Maurya BR and Verma JP. (2014). Does a rhizospheric microorganism enhance K+ availability in agricultural soils? *Microbiol. Res.*, 169(5): 337 – 347.

11) Padma SD and Sukumar J. (2015). Response of mulberry to inoculation of potash mobilizing bacterial isolate and other bio-inoculants. *Glob. J. Bio. Sci. Bio. Technol.*, 4: 50 – 53.

12) Parmar P and Sindhu SS. (2013). Potassium solubilization by rhizosphere bacteria: influence of nutritional and environmental conditions. *J. Microbiol. Res.*, 3(1): 25 – 31.

13) Prajapati K and Modi H. (2012). Isolation and characterization of potassium solubilizing bacteria from ceramic industry soil. *CIB Tech J. Microbiol.*, 1(2–3): 8 –14.

14) Rajawat MVS, Singh S, Tyagi SP and Saxena AK. (2016). A modified plate assay for rapid screening of potassium- solubilizing bacteria. *Pedosphere*, 26(5): 768 – 773.

15) Saha M, Maurya BR, Meena VS, Bahadur I and Kumar A. (2016). Identification and characterization of potassium solubilizing bacteria (KSB) from Indo-Gangetic Plains of India. *Biocatal. Agric. Biotechnol.*, 7: 202 - 209.

16) Saiyad SA, Jhala YK and Vyas RV. (2015). Comparative efficiency of five potash and phosphate solubilizing bacteria and their key enzymes useful for enhancing and improvement of soil fertility. *Int. J. Sci. Res. Publ.*, 5: 1 – 6.

17) Sheng X and Huang W. (2001). Mechanism of potassium release from feldspar affected by the sprain Nbt of silicate bacterium. *Acta Pedol Sin.*, 39(6): 863 – 871.

18) Sheng XF. (2005). Growth promotion and increased potassium uptake of cotton and rape by a potassium releasing strain of *Bacillus edaphicus. Soil Biol. Biochem.*, 37(10): 1918 – 1922.

19) Sindhu SS, Parmar P and Phour M. (2014). Nutrient cycling: potassium solubilization by microorganisms and improvement of crop growth. In: Geomicrobiology and Biogeochemistry. Springer, Berlin, pp 175–198.

20) Zhao S, Li K, Zhou W, Qiu S, Huang S and He P. (2016). Changes in soil microbial community, enzyme activities and organic matter fractions under long-term straw return in north Central China. *Agric. Ecosyst. Environ.*, 216: 82 – 88.